Town Land

by

J C Beswick

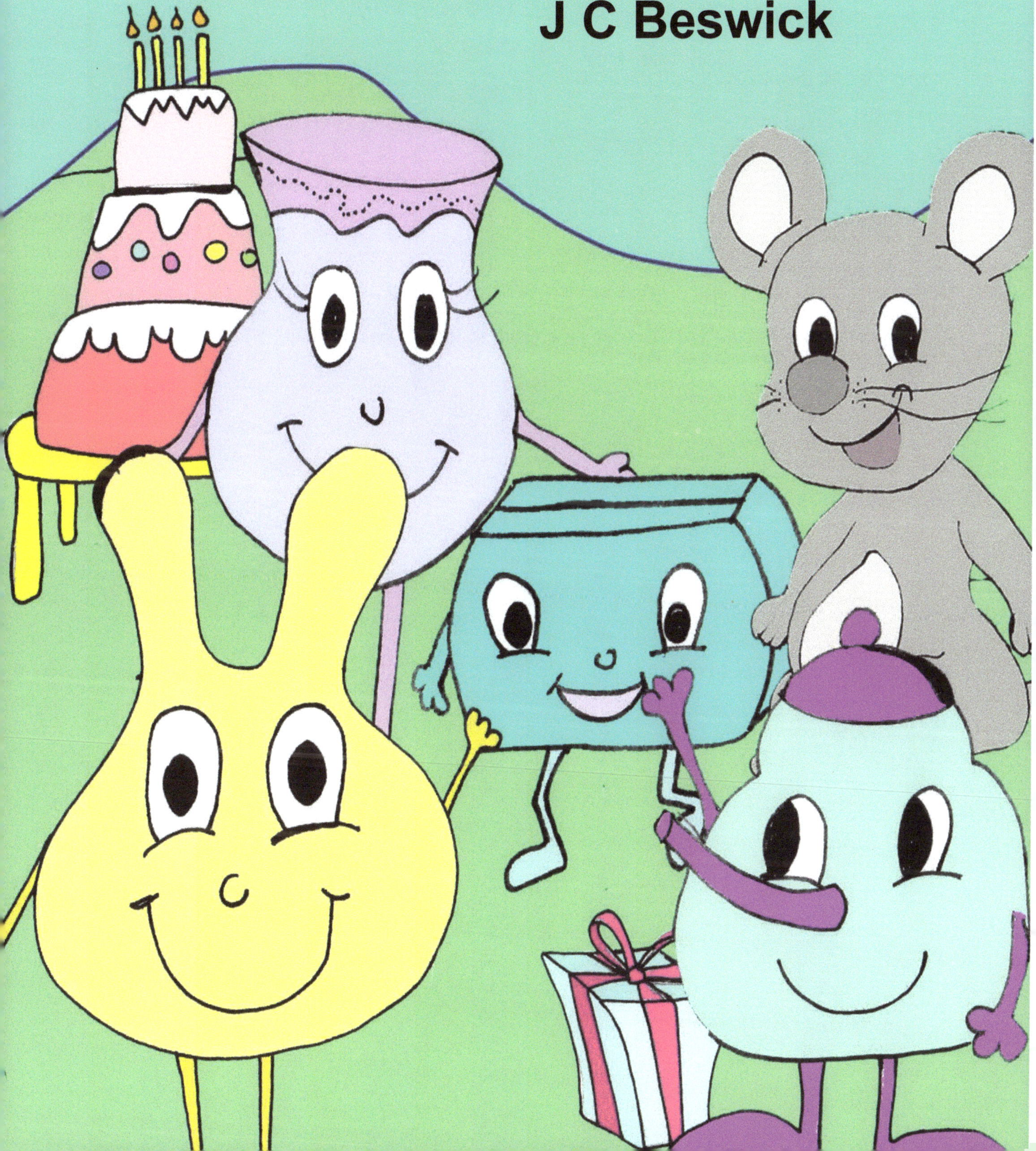

All rights reserved, no part of this publication may be reproduced by any means, electronic, mechanical photocopying, documentary, film or in any other format without prior written permission of the publisher.

Published by
Chipmunkapublishing
United Kingdom

http://www.chipmunkapublishing.com

Copyright ©   J C Beswick 2025

About Chipmunkapublishing

Mental health books give a voice to writers with mental illness around the world. At Chipmunkapublishing we raise awareness of mental health and the stigma surrounding mental health problems by encouraging society to listen. We are documenting mental health literature as a genre so history does not forget the survivors and carers of people with mental illness and disabilities.

About the Book

Bibby is a bib who has four best friends, Mr Kettle, Egg Cup, Toasty and Mr Mug. They all live in a small town called Small Town.

Which by the way is only one of the main places in Town Land, the other two popular parts are Big Town and the Town Land Park.

There are also other lands for example Magic Land. This book has thirty-one short different stories and pictures within so happy reading. Oh yes, try not read the stories at random for the first-time reading.

A Place Called Town Land

J C Beswick

Pictures by Julia Rusu

Author's Biography

The author James Cambell Beswick was born on 11th November 1978 in Cheltenham, Gloucestershire. He and his mother soon moved to Sutton Coldfield, West Midlands.

At the age of eleven diagnosed with dyslexia meaning there was a difficulty with reading and writing. As a result, a move from everyday schooling to a private school that specialised in helping dyslexics.

After one year there was a move back into mainstream education. In an additional same period off to a boarding school which could also support his study difficulties. When seventeen diagnosed with mental health.

What's Inside the Book

Rubbish Tip Wonder – Page 7 – 11

The Journey to the Fair – Page – 12 – 15

The Move – Page 16 – 19

Passing the Time – Page 20 – 23

Bibby's Ice Cream Shop – Page 24 – 27

A Bad Day at Work – Page 28 –30

Ghostly Things – Page 31 – 33

Bibby's Cousin Albert – Page 34 – 36

The Good Guys – Page 37 – 41

Train Day – Page 42 – 44

The Big Storm – Page 45 – 47

Parcel's New Friend – Page 48 – 51

Bibby goes on Holiday – Page 52 – 55

Magic Land – Page 56 – 59

The Small-Town Party – Page 60 – 62

The Clock – Page 63 – 66

The Circus comes to Town Land – Page 67 – 70

Water Park Fun – Page 71 – 74

The Return of the Good Guys – Page 75 – 78

Bibby's Lazy Day – Page 79 – 82

The Town Land Zoo – Page 83 – 85

Bob and Sam's Special Day – Page 86 – 88

Jammy, Jam, Jam – Page 89 – 92

Jumble, Jumble– Page 93 – 95

Bibby goes to Market – Page 96 – 99

Tug of War – Page 100 – 102

Home Help – Page 103 – 106

Soldier's Come to Town – Page 107 – 108

White Cloud Wonder – Page 111 – 114

Home Cooking – Page 115 – Page 117

Who is this? – Page 118 – Page 120

Rubbish Tip Wonder

Bibby, Egg Cup, Mr Kettle and Toasty looking for an adventure went over to the Big Town Rubbish Tip where they worked. Once there they built a space rocket for Bibby to fly around the stars.

When the rocket was made naming it HMS Rocket Ship Bibby opened its door, climbed in, and started the engines.

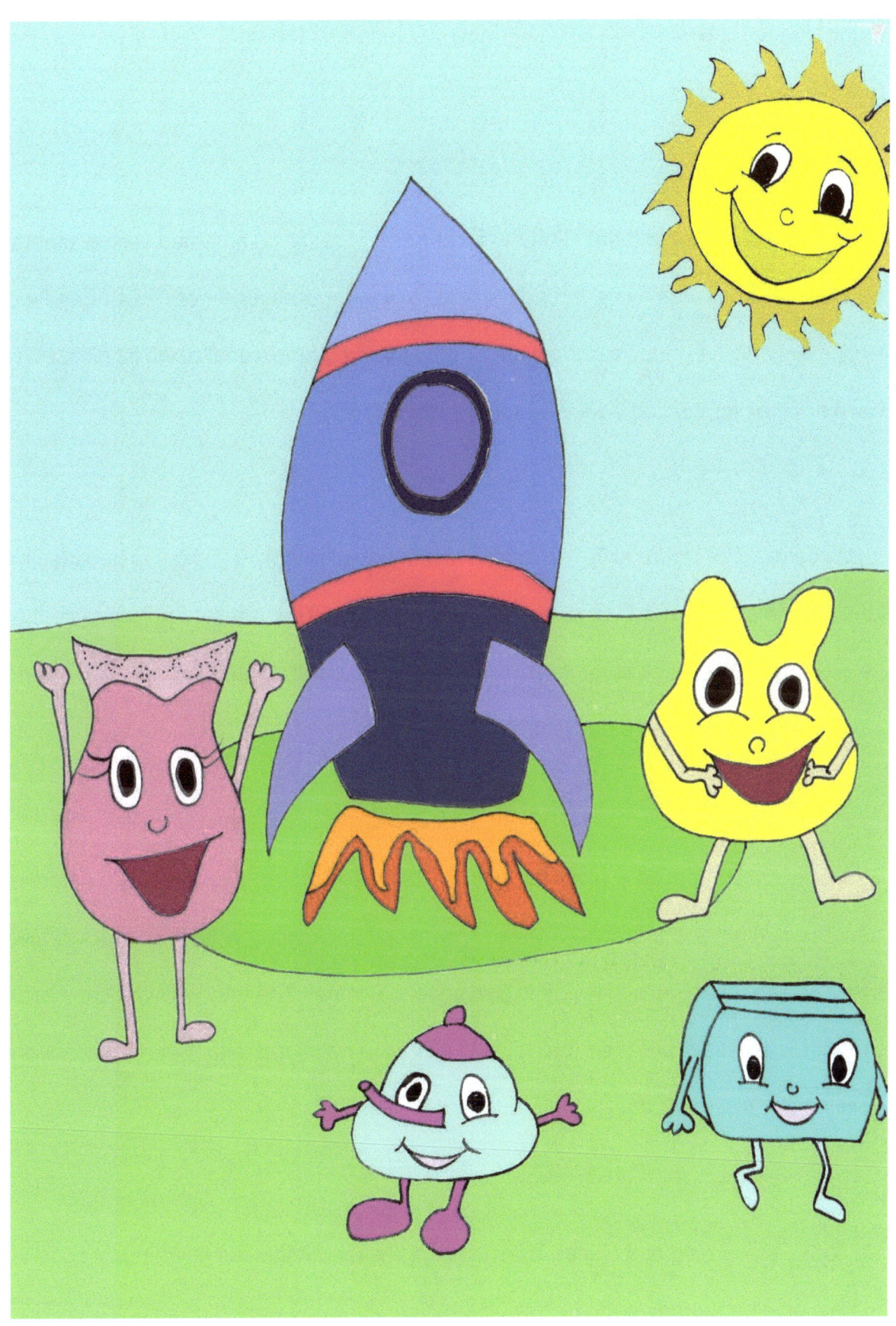

"It works." They cheered.

Bibby opened the window, "Space is now my friend till the end." With a whoosh the rocket was gone.

"It will be very quiet without Bibby around here." Toasty commented to the others. Meanwhile Bibby was flying through space. "I wonder if anyone from Town Land will miss me, I may be gone for some time." Bibby then remembered that whilst his friends were not looking, he had added a button onto the rocket.

It was called 'The return to Town Land in no time at all Button.' He did this because he knew that his Mum and Dad would defiantly miss him. Then he set the button so that he would get home five minutes from the moment he left. With it set he could spend as much time in space as he wanted.

Suddenly, Bibby noticed a small red planet. He typed into the space rocket's machine handbook 'What planet is this?' "Mars," the machine told him, "where the Mars people live. They are peaceful and loving to everyone they meet. The only way you can speak to them is by radio because their planet has no air and it is either very, hot or very cold." Bibby then radioed.

He spoke to the King and Queen who were impressed, "If there is anything, we can do to help on your journey we'll do it."

Bibby then used the handbook to find more planets. He noticed there were two more planets that he thought to himself, 'No one has ever probably seen these before.' They were called planet Sim and planet Trim. "Right then I'll go and see what they are like."

When arriving the two planets were awfully close together almost touching. He could also see two spaceships HMS Good and HMS Helper.

On HMS Good there was a space traveller called Mr Worm who was trying to help the people of planet Sim. On HMS Helper was another space traveller called Mr Mug. Trying to help the people of planet Trim. The reason they were helping was because the two planets were about to collide.

Bibby had an idea he radioed the King and Queen of Mars to see if they could help because the two planets were also just like Mars. They agreed. Before it was too late. The people from the planets that needed help were moved and lived happily forever.

But this story does not finish here. The space travellers were then invited by Bibby to come and live in Town Land.

"Where will we stay?"

"Mr Worm can move to the Town Land Park."

"What about Mr Mug?" Mr Worm questioned. "For Mr Mug it's the guesthouse in Small Town and he can work at the Rubbish Tip in Big Town."

The two then climbed into Bibby's spaceship. Bibby then pressed the 'Return to Town Land in no time at all Button.'

Five minutes later. They were home.

The Journey to the Fair

It was Friday. The following day Bibby and his friends were going to have a day off work. Bibby suggested, "Shall we go to the Big Town Fair tomorrow?"

"We'd love to go but isn't the journey to the Fair a bit scary to say the least?"

"Trust me." They then arranged to meet the following morning.

The next day was beautiful. Really hot and sunny. As it usually is in Town Land. The way they were going to go was past the Big Pond, along the Blue River, over the Town Land Bridge and then through the Grumpy Farmers' Field.

They set off. When the five arrived at the Big Pond Bibby dived in followed by his friends. They stayed there swimming and having fun. Then dried themselves in the sun before moving on.

Next, they came to the Blue River. It was blue, clear, and full of fish. Their friends used to live here but moved out years ago.

As they walked along the edge of the Blue River Toasty began to rummage around in the long grass, "I have left a fishing rod around here somewhere. Let us fish for a while." They took it in turns to fish. After some time and with no joy in catching anything, they continued their journey.

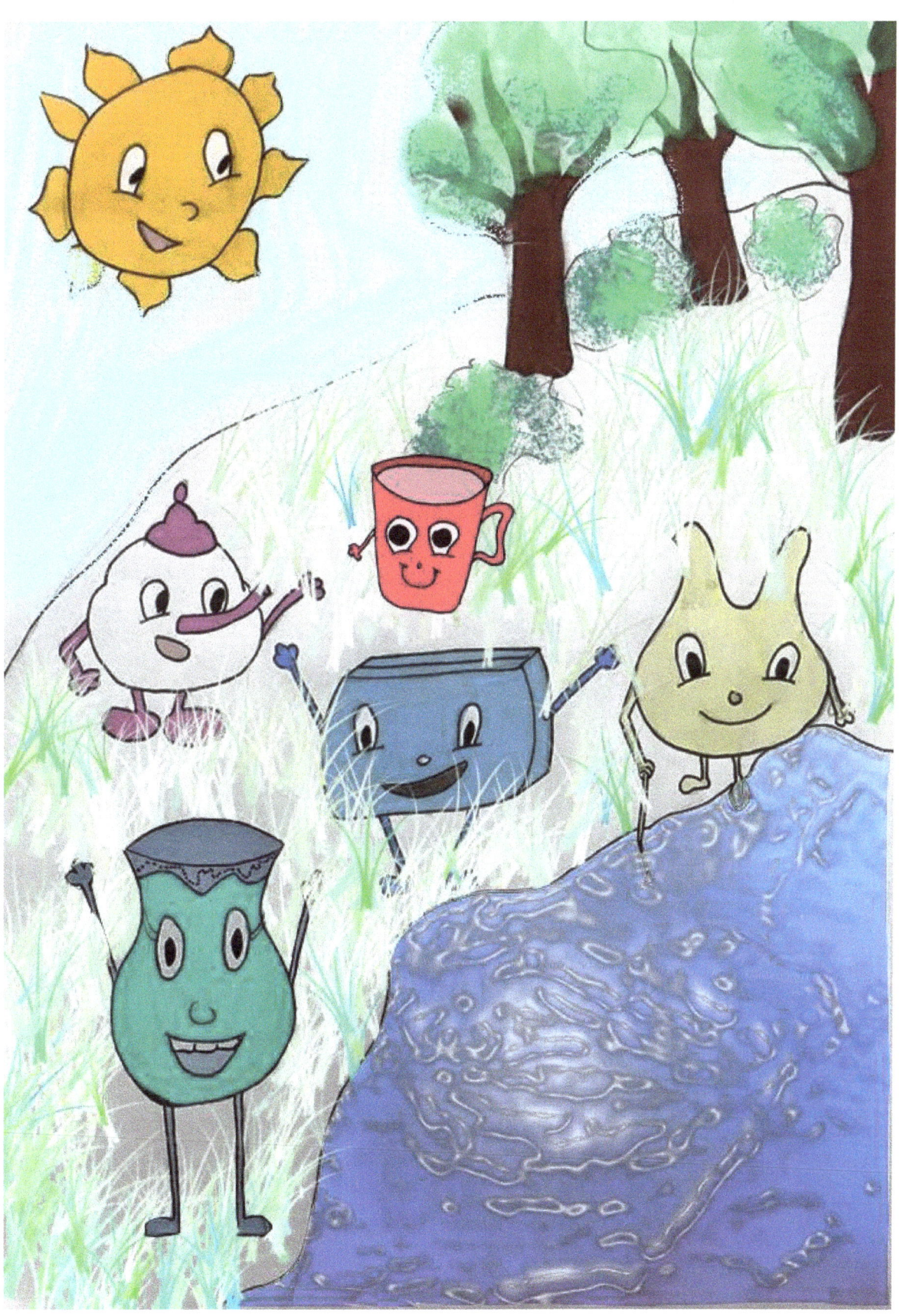

Crossing the Town Land Bridge, they came to the edge of the Farmers' Field. On the other side of the field the Grumpy Farmer could be seen stacking hay onto his hay stacking truck.

This Farmer was the grumpiest man in the world. He hated people in his field. They began to run through. "Hey! Get out of my field!" He shouted grumpily. Turning his truck towards them.

Luckily though, they had made it safely to the other side. The Farmer turned his truck around in a full circle and went back to work. Two minutes later they arrived at the Fair.

It was very, busy. There was music playing, flashing lights and lots of rides to play on. Bibby and his friends made sure they went on every ride. They had candyfloss and ate burgers. Unfortunately, soon it was time to go and journey back to Bibby's house. Reaching there safely as they had decided to go the long way home.

The Move

In a hole in the ground lives a quiet shy mouse called Little Mr Mouse. He had lived there under the Big Town Post Office in Big Town for an awfully long time. Little Mr Mouse decided one day that it was time to move. But where he did not know, 'I think I'll visit Bibby and ask him where's best,' he thought to himself.

"The Town Land Park."

"Yes, because there I can have the biggest home ever. I will ask Bob, Sam and Mr Kettle to help me move."

Little Mr Mouse went straight around to the Post Office to see Bob and Sam. Collecting boxes for his belongings, tape to seal the boxes and a van to move his things.

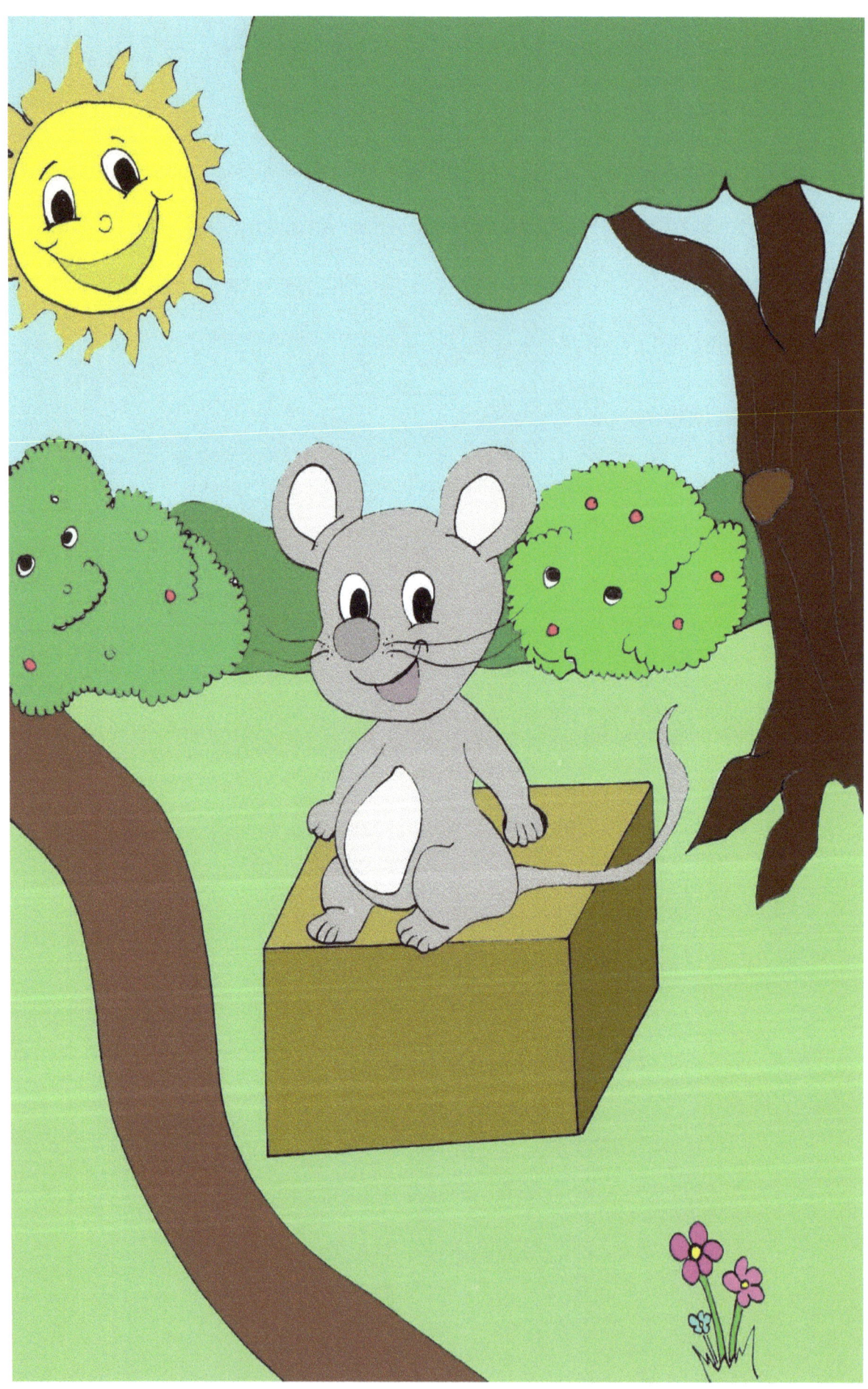

A few days later Little Mr Mouse had packed, and everything was ready to be moved. The next day he told Bob, "Put that box on the top please." It was the largest box. Suddenly it came tumbling down from the van. Onto the floor with a crash and a bang.

Oh, dear Little Mr Mouse was not happy. Fortunately, nothing was broken just the box. Quickly everything was put into a new one. Sealed with tape and safely put onto the van. "Off we go." He said over the moon with joy.

Mr Kettle who was sitting at the back of the van piped up saying, "So, where is your new home going to be at the park?"

"Umm, I don't know yet."

"Okay. I'm sure it will be a good choice and a fine home."

Arriving and in no time Little Mr Mouse found a place. It was under the Old Oak Tree in the centre of the park. He began to dig. The digging went on and on.

By that evening his home was almost finished. The sun had gone down, and he started to unpack slowly settling in. Sitting down he thought to himself, 'How could I thank my friends for helping me?' As he began to think he soon realised, "I know. I will have a home warming party."

PTO

The next day he invited over those that had helped. Arranging for his friends to meet at his later. He prepared delicious food and made soft drinks.

That evening the helpers arrived and enjoyed the food and drink. Everyone was extremely pleased indeed.

Passing the Time

The weather was hot, and it was getting hotter and hotter. Bibby and his friends were cleaning their house windows. Soon it was too hot to do anything. "Shall we have some ice cream to cool us down?" Eggcup suggested.

"Egg-cellent idea." They replied.

The idea of sitting in the sun and eating ice cream seemed wonderful. Eggcup went straight to his house to get some. When he returned, they sat down and ate and ate.

"Shall we put up Mr Kettle's paddling pool in his back garden?" Toasty asked.

"What a brilliant idea." Mr Mug commented joyfully.

Once moved too Mr Kettles they set up the pool. Filling it full of water. Climbing in slowly because the water was cold. They splashed, played, and had the time of their lives. Before long, a water fight broke out.

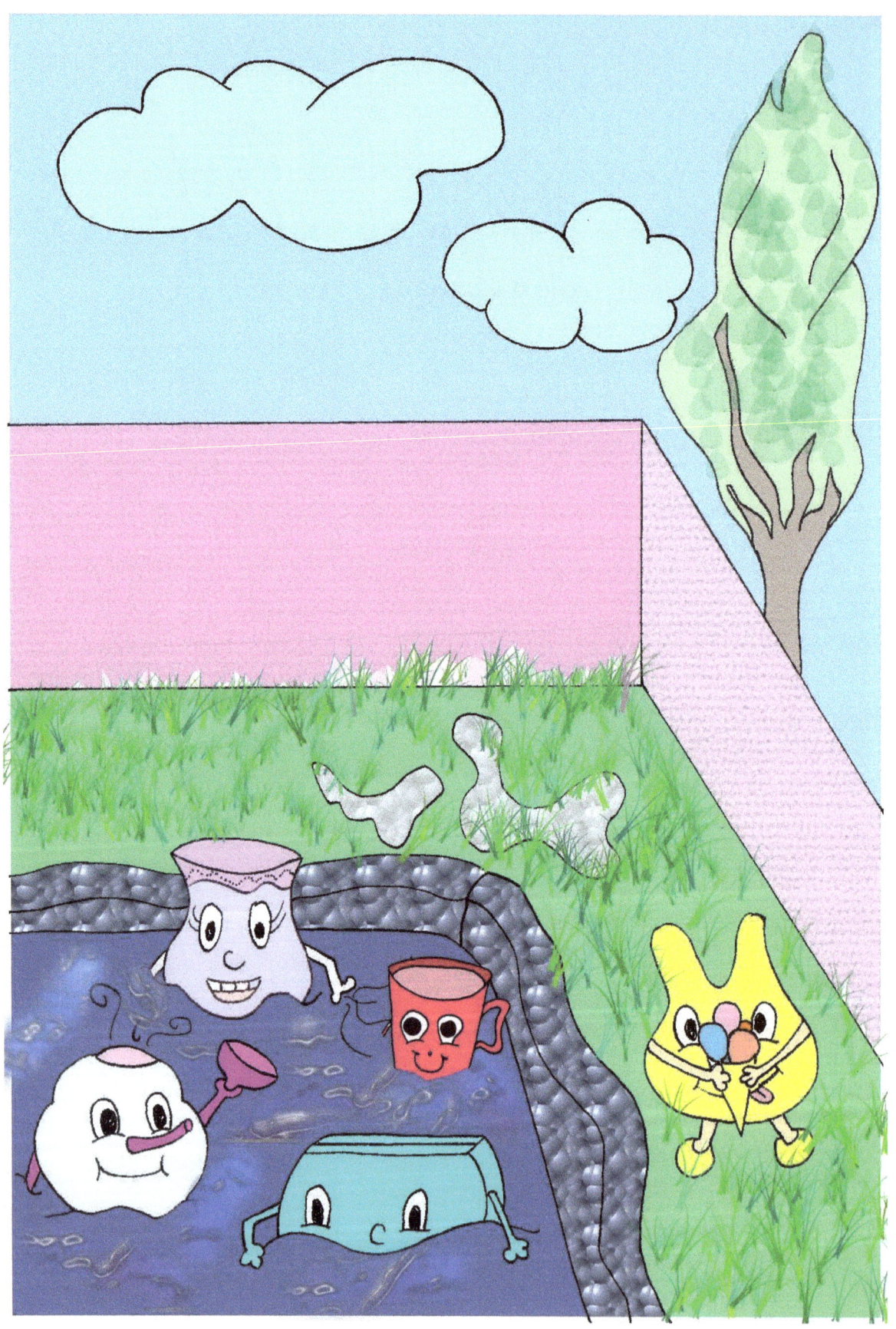

Bang! A noise came from Mr Mugs' house next door. The five friends became frightened. They did not understand why there was a noise coming from the empty house. As they looked over the fence. They saw something fly past one of the windows.

"Why don't we go over and find out what's going on." Bibby said.

"We're too scared." The four replied. Their eyes wide with fright. But before anyone could act. They noticed the front door opening.

"I know what that is," Toasty said, "it's a parcel. It must have run away from the Big Town Post Office where Bob and Sam work."

Mr Kettle agreed, "Town Land parcels can be difficult at times. They have minds of their own. Let us get Bob and Sam here to help."

Bibby could not wait for them to arrive. He walked over to the parcel. The others could not bear to look. Moving closer and closer soon Bibby was standing right in front of the parcel.

The parcel trembling with fear could hardly get its words out. "PPPPlease don't hurt me."

"Don't worry I won't."
"I was hoping to move into this house, I thought you might stop me, so I tried to run away, and I knocked over some things. I'm sorry."

"What's your name?"

"Parcel."

"Don't worry Parcel. I think I may be able to help you I just need to speak with my friends a moment."

Bibby then went to tell the others about Parcel's problem. With a chat they decided it would be best to build Parcel a home of his own near to the Big Town Fair. Telling Parcel their plan he was delighted. Over the next few days Bibby and his friends did just that.

Bibby's Ice Cream Shop

Bibby had built himself an Ice Cream Shop right in the middle of Big Town. He was tired of working at the Big Town Rubbish Tip. His four friends helped him to build the shop. It was tall, colourful and had loads of different flavoured ice creams to sell. Bibby had built it just in time for the hot weather.

"Bye," the four said, "have fun at your new job today." Bibby set off on his way. He arrived. Unlocked the doors. Then began to wait for customers to arrive. He waited and waited. No one came. It was soon three o'clock but still no one had come to his shop. He shut the shop and headed home.

When he got home, he decided to take a nap. Setting his alarm for six as he remembered he was going to his Mum and Dad's house for dinner. Whilst he was sleeping people started to arrive at the shop. Only to find that it was closed.

Beep, beep, beep went his alarm. He jumped out of bed. 'Right time for some dinner,' he thought to himself. With that he set off for his parent's. "Hi Mum, hi Dad." They seemed very cross. Not knowing what was wrong he sat down waiting for his dinner. They began to eat. There was total silence.

After dinner was finished Bibby's Dad asked in a loud voice, "Why was the Ice Cream Shop shut today?" Straight away Bibby realized what he had done.

"Oh no what can I do to put this right," Quickly he stood up, "tell all of Town Land the shop will be open in no time." He then ran over to Big Town and opened it. Soon people found out that the shop was now open.

In no time the shop started to get busy. Bibby was very, happy. Then as it got quieter Mr Kettle arrived. "Please can I have a chocolate and toffee ice cream would you like one as well Bibby?"

"I'd love one."

PTO

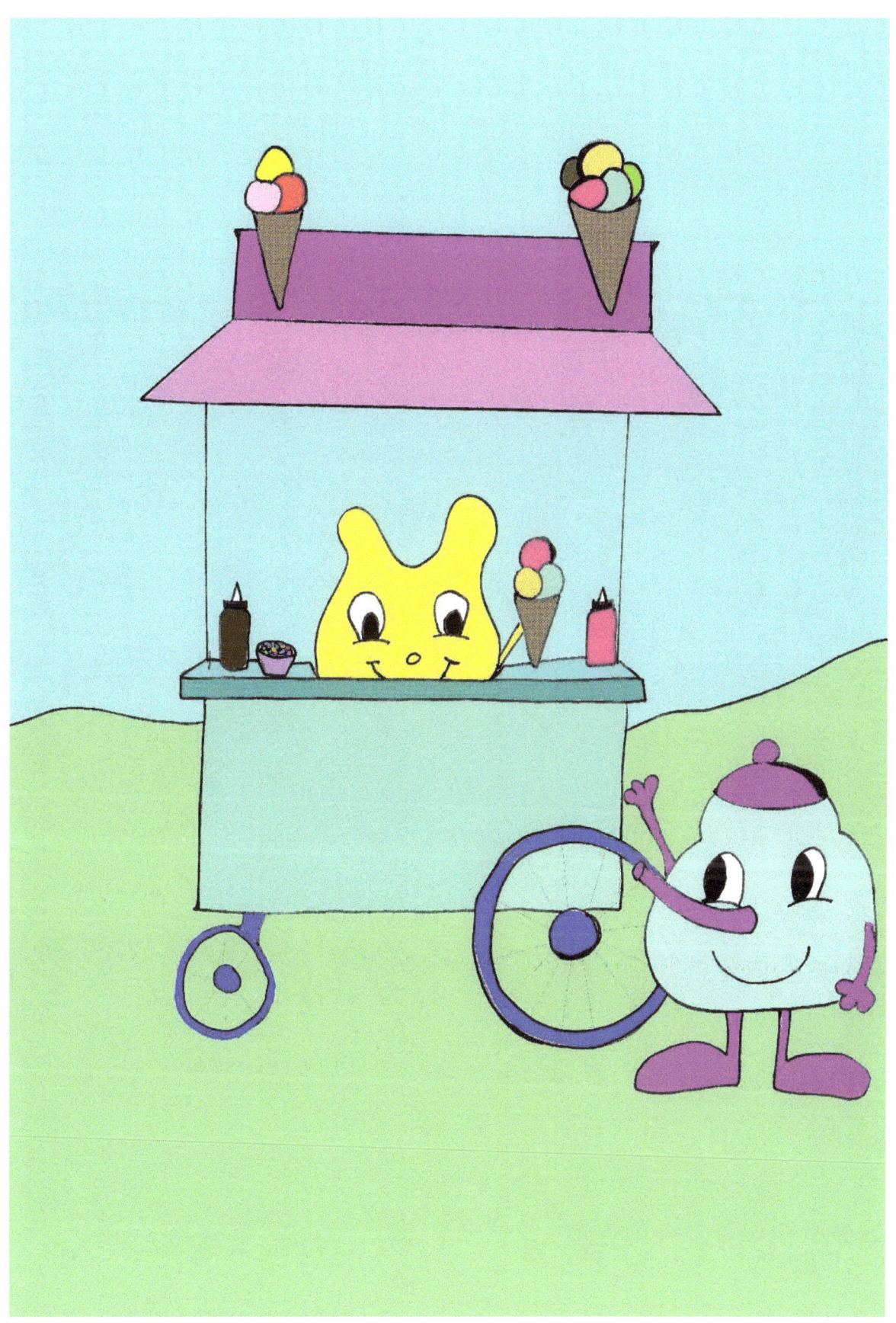

PTO

Bibby then gave Mr Kettle his ice cream. As Bibby went to eat his parents walked in. "You've just had your dinner I'll have that." His Mum said as she whipped it from his hand. Mr Kettle began to laugh.

As the shop was a hit with everyone Bibby was as proud as punch.

A Bad Day at Work

Bibby's parents Mr and Mrs Bib who live and work at the Big Town's Fish and Chip Shop was about to have a bad day. Paying them a visit was somebody from Mega Mess Land who is very, very messy indeed.

The Mega Mess people were the messiest people ever. Things were bound to get messy. If you have ever been to Mega Mess Land you would quickly realise that you weren't too messy at all.

"Hello, morning both." Mega Messman said.

"Hello, would you like some dinner?"

"Of course."

"That's no problem."

The two then set to work. That evening he came back to the shop. "Hi there, is the food ready please?"

"Of course." Mrs Bib answered as she put the last portion with the others.

"Thank you." With that he paid and picked up the wrappings of food. Turning he began to walk out of the shop. As he did so he sneezed. Oh no, mess everywhere.

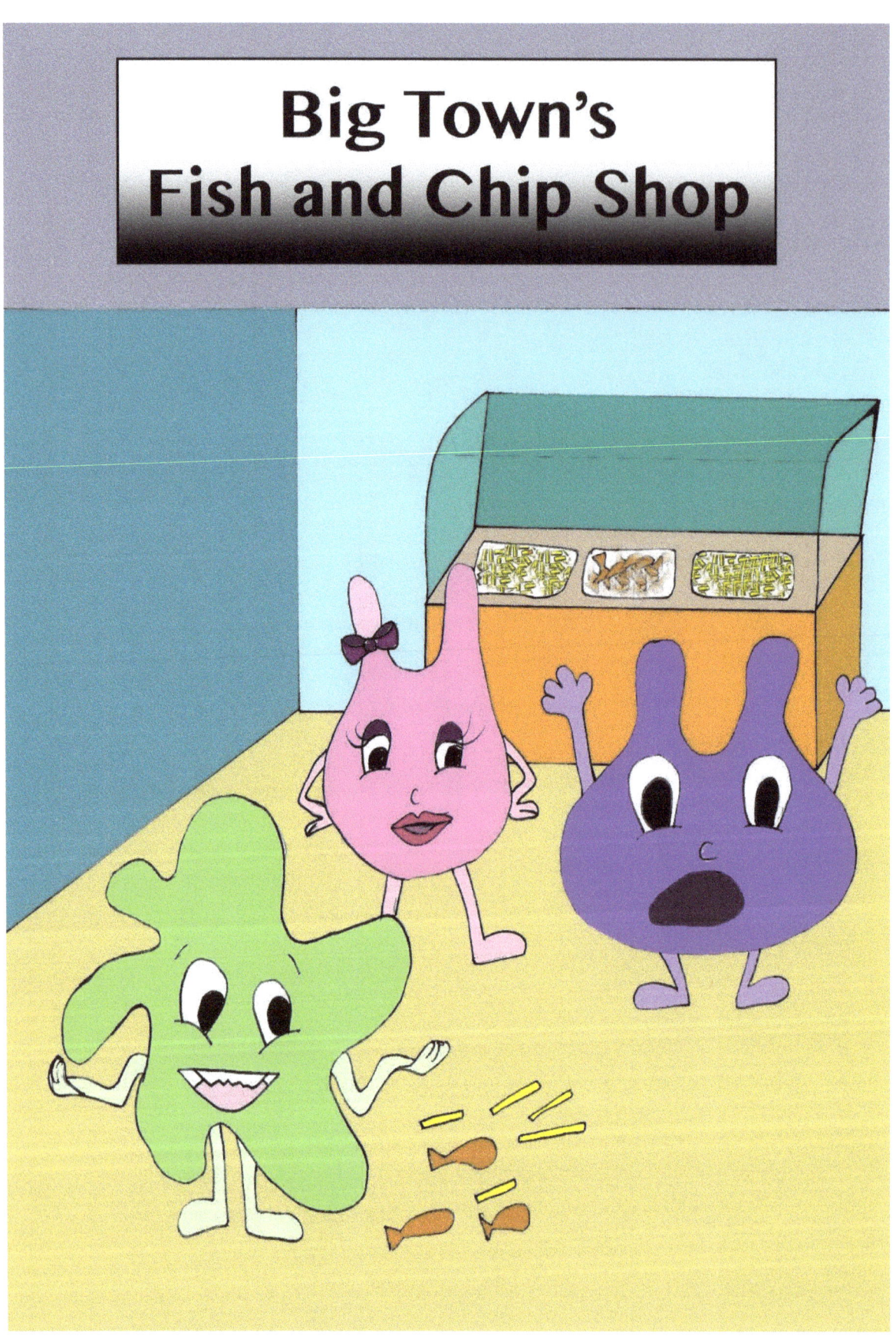

He stood up. As he did this, he began to tread all over the now unwrapped meals. Sneezing as he did so. The two could not believe what they were seeing. Quickly, they went over to help.

"What have I done?"

"Don't worry we will bring fresh over soon." After all it was not quite mealtime.

"Thank you again." He said cleaning himself down setting off back to Mega Mess Land.

Later that evening just in time for everyone to be hungry. Mr and Mrs Bib arrived with dinner.

Ghostly Things

Shelly and Mr Ghost are friendly ghosts and live in Big Town. One day they decided to get married. They wanted to have the Reverend Robinson marry them at the Big Town Church. As they thought it was beautiful.

Getting married meant everything to them. They only wanted a small wedding. So, the two invited Samuel and Sanford who were also ghosts.

The church was noticeably big. With lots of glass windows and a huge church organ. The two invited friends decorated the church. This took three days and looked lovely.

"I hope they will like the flowers and paper chains?" Samuel wondered.

"I'm sure they will."

Buying the wedding presents was the next thing on the guests list of things to do. Samuel bought a garden table with two chairs. Sanford bought gardening tools. As the wedding couple loved gardening.

Shelly and Mr Ghost decided they would invite every member of Town Land after the wedding for a party.

The big day arrived. The Bride and Groom looked happy as can be. They walked into the church seeing the flowers and paper chains. Then the Reverend married them. They then walked down the aisle, out the church doors and had confetti thrown all over them.

They then returned home as Mr and Mrs Ghost. Where their invited guests were waiting with cards and presents. The gifts were opened, and food was eaten. Then they all danced and sang late into the evening.

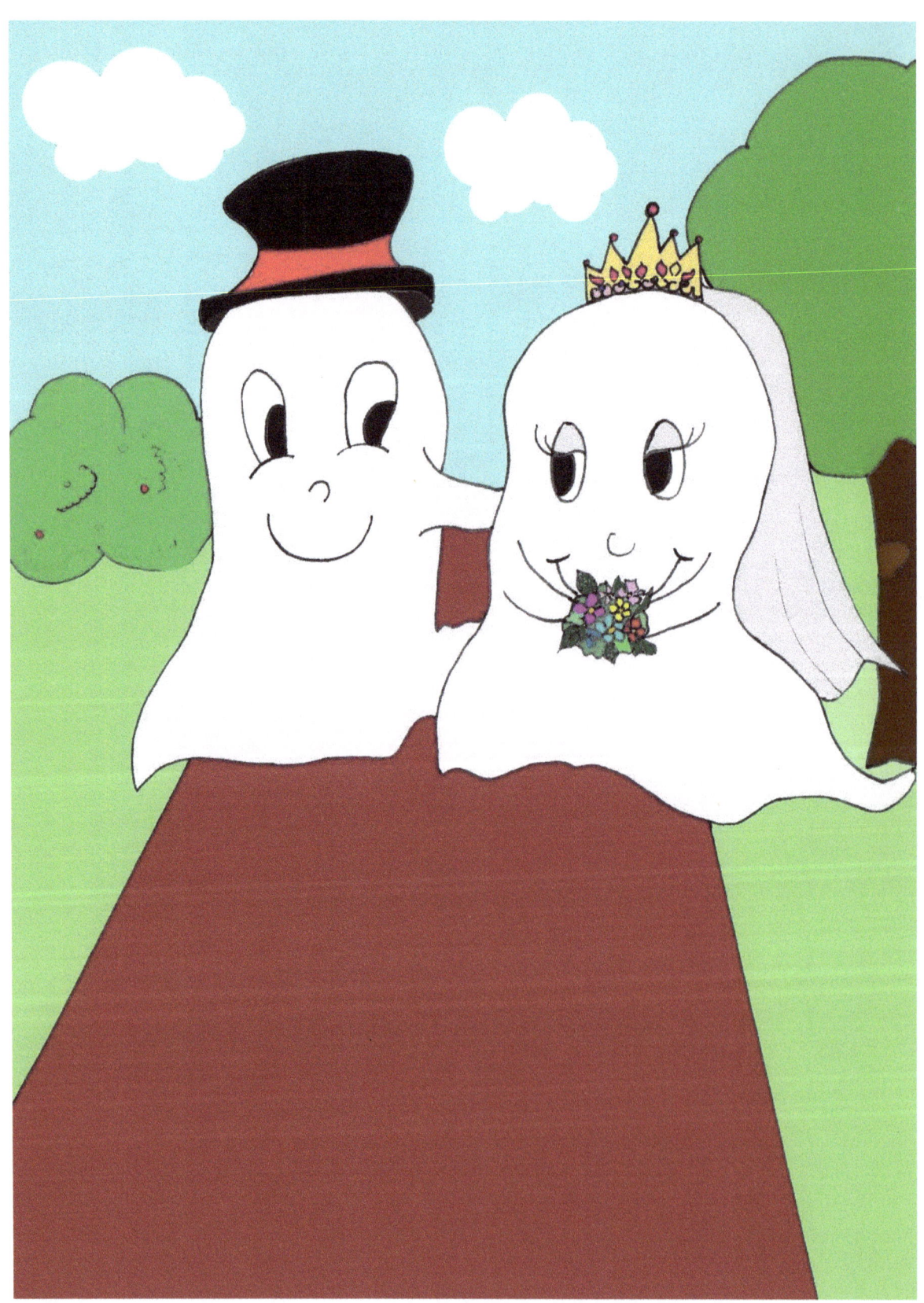

Bibby's Cousin Albert

Albert wanted to get a new job. So, he went to see the Grumpy Farmer not knowing anything about the Farmer and his four workers. Fred, Rita, Darton and Teddy. If you did not know the Farmer and his works were the grumpiest people in the world. Even on good days.

"Good morning." Albert politely greeted them.

"What do you want!?" The Farmer replied.

"I am looking for work."

"Why are you bothering us?" Albert shook in his boots.

"I would really like to work for you."

"Right! I will give you work! Go and put the pigs away, collect the hen's eggs and tidy up the hay up!"

All day long the Farmer shouted orders at Albert. Whilst the others did nothing. At the end of the day the Farmer told Albert to go home. He went home tired, hungry, and thirsty.

As Albert was just about to sit down with a drink and some food. There was a knock at his door, "Hi," it was Bibby, "I have come to offer you a new job."

"I already have one."

"Where?"

"At the Grumpy Farmer's Farm."

"Umm, I think we need to have a little chat," the two then chatted for a long time, "do you realise that the Grumpy Farmer may not even pay you."

"I think I would like to work at the job you have for me."

"Yes, but first I think it's time to teach the Farmer and his workers a lesson. Did they say what they are doing tomorrow first thing?"

"Yes, they're cleaning the stables."

The next day Albert went to work as normal. Pretending nothing was going to happen. The grumps could be heard from the stables moaning about him. Not knowing what was in store. Suddenly, there was a scream. Before they knew what was happening a farm of pigs, hens and cows were heading towards them.

"What's going on!?" They screamed. Once inside the stable the animals got frightened and started snapping.

"Ouch." A mischievous piglet had bitten the Farmer on the bottom. Hens were flying everywhere. Cows were mooing loudly.

In the commotion they ran out of the stables screaming. As they did so they frightened the horses. "Come on let's go." Bibby and the friends ran back to his house laughing and laughing the whole day long.

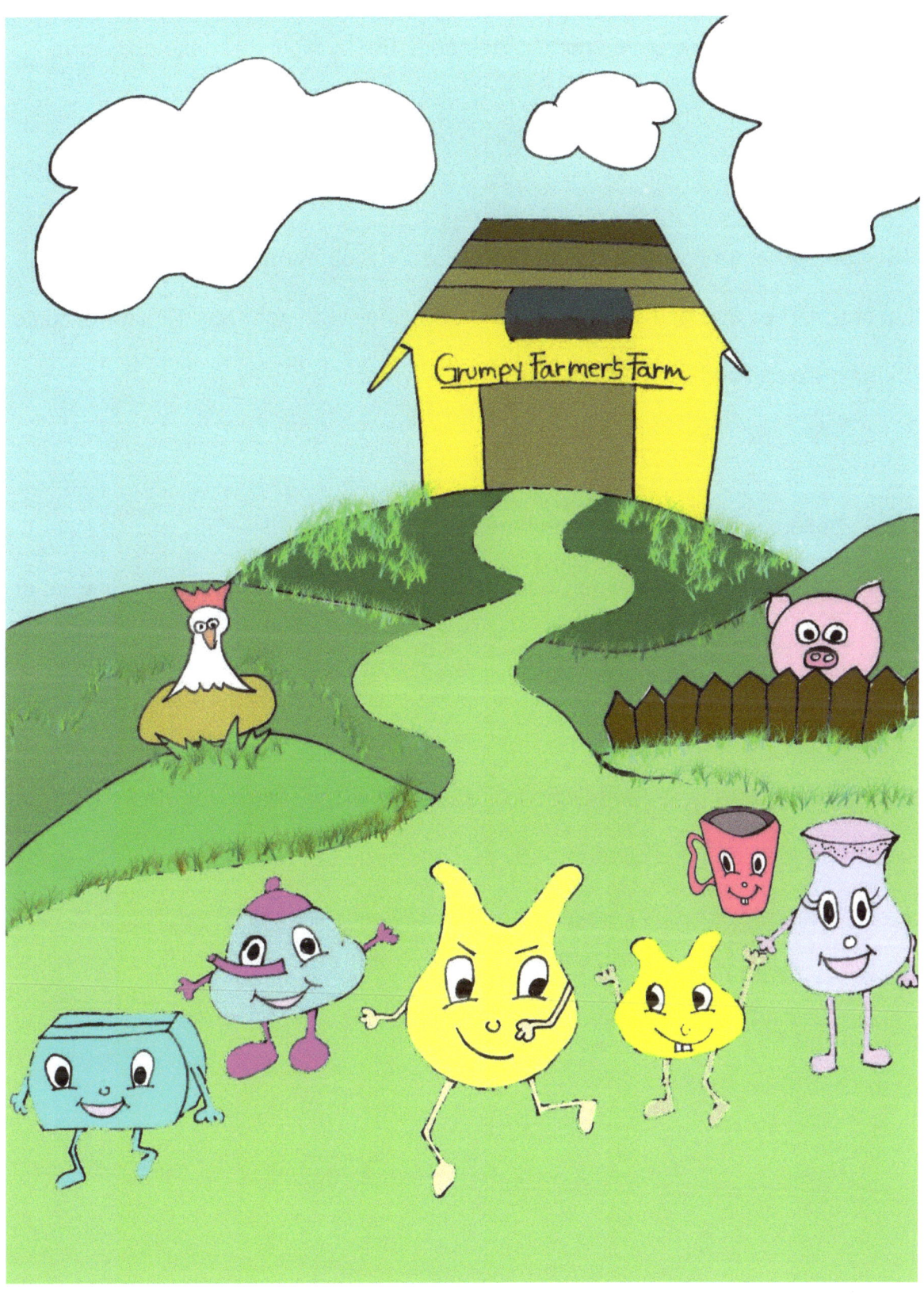

The Good Guys

Town Land like Earth has its own superheroes and villains. In the daytime the good and bad guys were known as normal members. But by night they take on secret identities.

The good guys are none other than Mrs Colson, Jacob, Kirby, and Chester the Labrador. They live and work at the Big Town Fair. By night Mrs Colson becomes Captain Colson and she is the leader.

Jacob becomes Jet Set Jacob. Kirby becomes Cape Crusader Kirby and Chester the Labrador becomes Chester the Chocolate Coloured Labrador. Their superpowers are that they need no sleep, and nothing can harm them if Town Land is safe.

Darton, Fred, Rita, and Teddy who live and work at the Grumpy Farmers Farm are known as the bad guys. Darton becomes Dastardly Darton Dark who is the leader, Fred becomes Ferocious Forever Fred, Rita becomes Raging Rotten Rita and Teddy becomes Teddy Time.

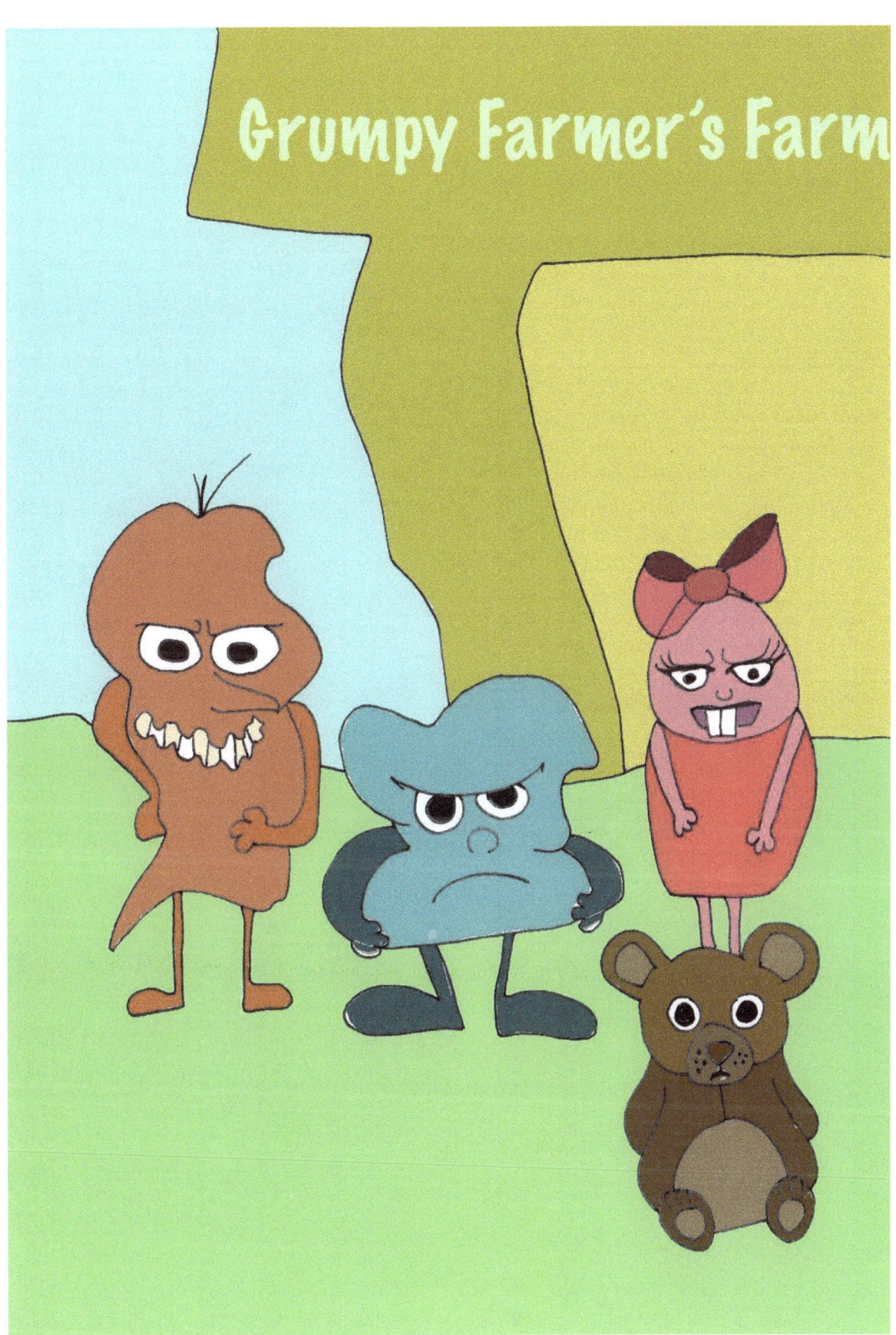

They too have powers as well. Like the superheroes they need no sleep, but in this case each of their powers are different.

Dastardly Darton Dark can put things into darkness, Ferocious Forever Fred can make things last forever, Raging Rotten Rita can make things rotten and Teddy Time can do things with time.

The story begins one day whilst Darton was working on the farm. He began thinking about a dastardly plan. That evening he had changed and had gathered his fellows to a meeting.

"I have a plan together we can put the whole of Town Land into a world of darkness forever and make it rotten. Ridding us of Captain Colson and her men."

They continued with the plan late into the night. It was soon morning. By this time, they had made a machine that would make the plan go ahead. Little did they know though that whilst making the plan in a passage under their base sat Chester the Chocolate Coloured Labrador listening to every word.

Unlike them the superheroes were smart. They knew that if they did not keep an eye on the bad guys that things could go horribly wrong. Chester ran straight back to the base.

"Captain Colson, Captain Colson!" He shouted, "Dastardly's up to no good again."

"What's he up to this time we must make a plan."

That coming evening the four began to plan how to stop the evil from going ahead and hopefully destroy the others' powers. By early morning they planned to make a reverse draining switch and attach it onto the machine.

The next morning Town Land went about his and her day as normal. But soon it was night fall again.

"It is time," Dastardly Darton Dark ordered, "switch on the machine."

"Not so fast." Captain Colson shouted.

"That's what you think turn the machine to full power."

"You fool." Cape Crusader Kirby chuckled.

"Do it now." The machine was switched to full power.

With the superhero's switch at the top of the bad guys, machine it was clear what was going to happen next. Almost straight away the evil powers of the four were no more.

Captain Colson and her men had done it. Town Land was saved. The next morning Darton, Fred, Rita and Teddy went to work at the Grumpy Farmers Farm with an incredibly good reason to be grumpy.

Train Day

There was a special train visiting Town Land for the first time. This train was not like normal ones. It was different because it would put its own track down as it went to new places.

Town Land was enjoying a normal peaceful day. When suddenly, there was a bang and a clang, a chuff and a choo. The train stopped right outside Bibby's house.

PTO

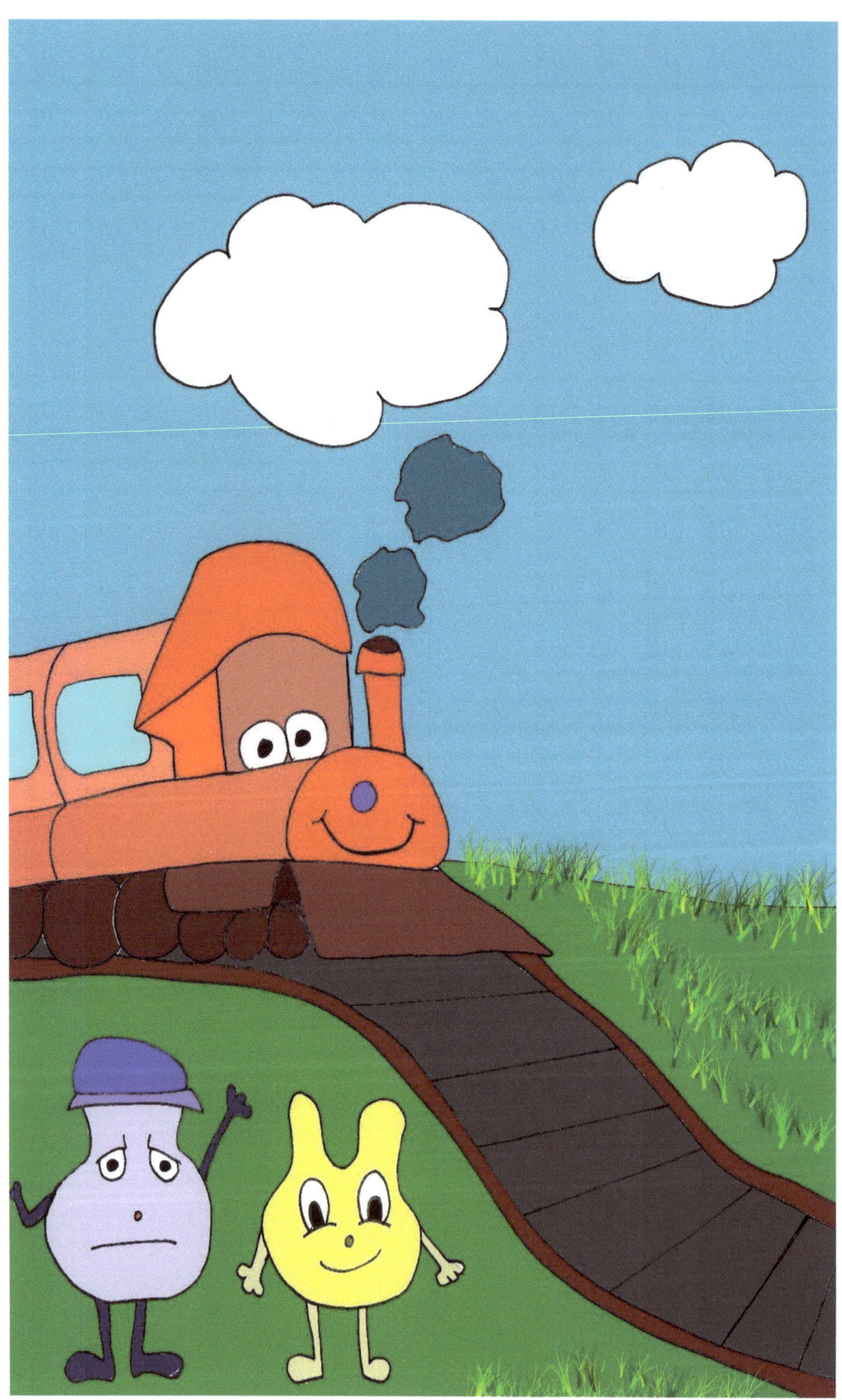

Bibby had heard all about the train and the Train Man. Bibby was chuffed to bits to see him. The Train Man was from Train Land and the people there were called the Train People.

"Hello, nice to see you Bibby."

"Why are you here?" Bibby questioned.

"I have a small problem with my train. When it is putting track down it keeps going over to the right. I have had to go all over the place just to get here. Can you help me to fix it please?"

"I'm sorry to hear that. Of course, I will help you." Bibby then went to get his friends to help. They lifted the train up onto Bibby's Special Train Fixing Machine which he had made just in case there was ever a problem.

They began to mend the train, "It'll be fixed in no time." Eggcup told the Train Man.

"Brilliant how can I repay you?"

"Well, there's one small job that we need you to do." Bibby asked.

"Please tell me. I'll do it."

"Can you lay down train track, then we can build trains and stations?"

"No problem, Bibby. I'll do it right away."

Before long, the Town Land Railway was complete, and everyone was happy.

The Big Storm

The leaves on the trees were orange and brown, and nearly ready to fall off. A strong wind began to blow across the land. Beginning at the Town Land Park and heading towards Small Town.

The Old Oak Tree's leaves began to blow away in the wind. Little Mr Mouse closed up the entrance to his house, sat in front of his log fire with a cup of tea and began to wait for the storm to pass.

Soon the stormy air began to blow over Small Town followed by rain. Before long it was raining badly. "Inside the Guesthouse quickly," Bibby suggested to his friends, "light the fire. We must dry off because we will catch colds."

In no time the storm had almost reached Big Town. "There's a big storm heading towards us." Mr Bib warned Mrs Bib. The weather was getting colder, windier, and wetter by the minute. As the rain continued to pour down, the Big Pond and the Blue River were almost overflowing.

The next day the storm was still in full swing. Little Mr Mouse had spent the night in front of his fire as he had fallen asleep. Waking and walking towards the entrance of his home. He could still hear the wind and could feel the cold outside. Quickly he decided to go back to the warmth of the fire.

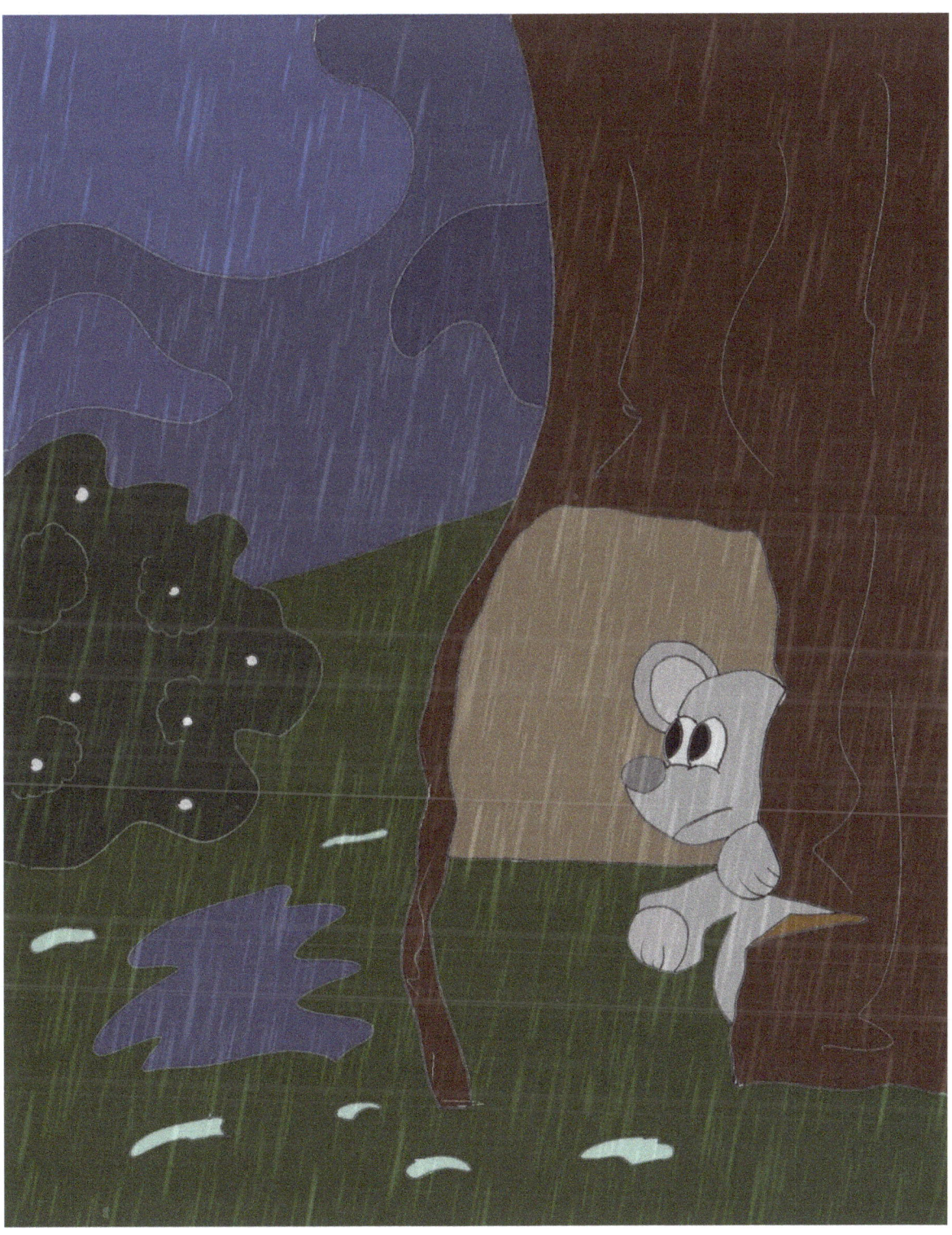

Back at the Guesthouse in Small Town Bibby and his four friends were pillow fighting having the time of their lives.

Over in Big Town the Reverend Robinson and the Grumpy Farmer were not impressed at all. That night the Reverend had spent the whole evening changing buckets of rainwater. The Farmer had spent the whole night calming down the horses because of the noise from the gale.

By the following day, the storm had gone, and Town Land was nearly back too normal. Bibby had talked his friends into staying over at the Guesthouse. What they should have been doing though was covering over the rubbish at the tip.

"Come on let's go and tidy." Mr Mug said to the friends.

By the time, the five arrived. To their surprise Mr and Mrs Bib were already there, "I'm glad you are all here because the rubbish still needs covering up." Mrs Bib crossly told them.

Before long, the mess was swept up and covered over. At last Town Land was back too normal at least until next year perhaps.

Parcel's New Friend

It was Little Mr Mouse's birthday. Parcel had arranged to meet his friends and then walk up too Little Mr Mouse's house with them. Setting off to meet his friends he stopped. Looking over the gate at the Grumpy Farmer's Farmhouse, 'I'm not going in there they're too grumpy.' Parcel thought to himself and then continued, on his way.

Parcel was soon at the Big Town Fish and Chip Shop where he had arranged to meet everyone. He pushed open the doors and walked in. "Hello," he said. There was no reply. "Hello." There was still no reply. Parcel thought that his friends must be at the Big Town Shop where Gran and Granddad Bib live and work. He continued, on his journey.

Parcel arrived at the shop and put his head around the door. "Hello," nobody answered. "Hello." He called again there was still no answer.

'Funny there's no one at the Fish and Chip Shop and no one here. What is going on,' he wondered, "I know everyone must be at Little Mr Mouse house." Parcel then carried on his way. He arrived at Little Mr Mouse's. Only to find that there was also no one there.

Parcel knelt at the edge of the doorway. "Hello Happy Birthday," there was no response, "is anybody there?" He was now starting to get upset believing that everyone was trying to avoid him. He decided to walk over to the Big Pond.

As he walked, he started to cry. Arriving at the pond he sat down at the edge. He cried and cried. As the tears ran down his face, he rubbed his eyes. "Nobody likes me. I have tried to find my friends. Do I have any friends in this land?" Suddenly, there was a rustle in the long grass near to where he was sat.

Parcel leant over parting the long grass. Right before him was another parcel. Who then began to speak, "Hello my name is Tommie what's yours?"

"No one likes me. So, you'd better not speak to me Tommie."

"I haven't got any friends either."

"Parcel's my name."

"Oh, dear hang on I think I may be able to help you, everyone is at Bibby's house today. He was meant to tell you where they were."

"How do you know this?"

"I overheard them talking at the Post Office."

"Thank you so much. Bibby must have forgotten to tell me. I know you can be my friend. You can live at my house and I'll take you with me to the party if you like?"

"Yes please."

With their newfound friendship. Both then journeyed to Bibby's house. When they arrived, Bibby ran up to Parcel. "I'm sorry. I forgot to tell you. I went everywhere looking for you."

"Don't worry. I am here now. Meet my new friend Tommie."

Bibby welcomed Tommie taking him to meet his friends, they then had the best time ever.

PTO

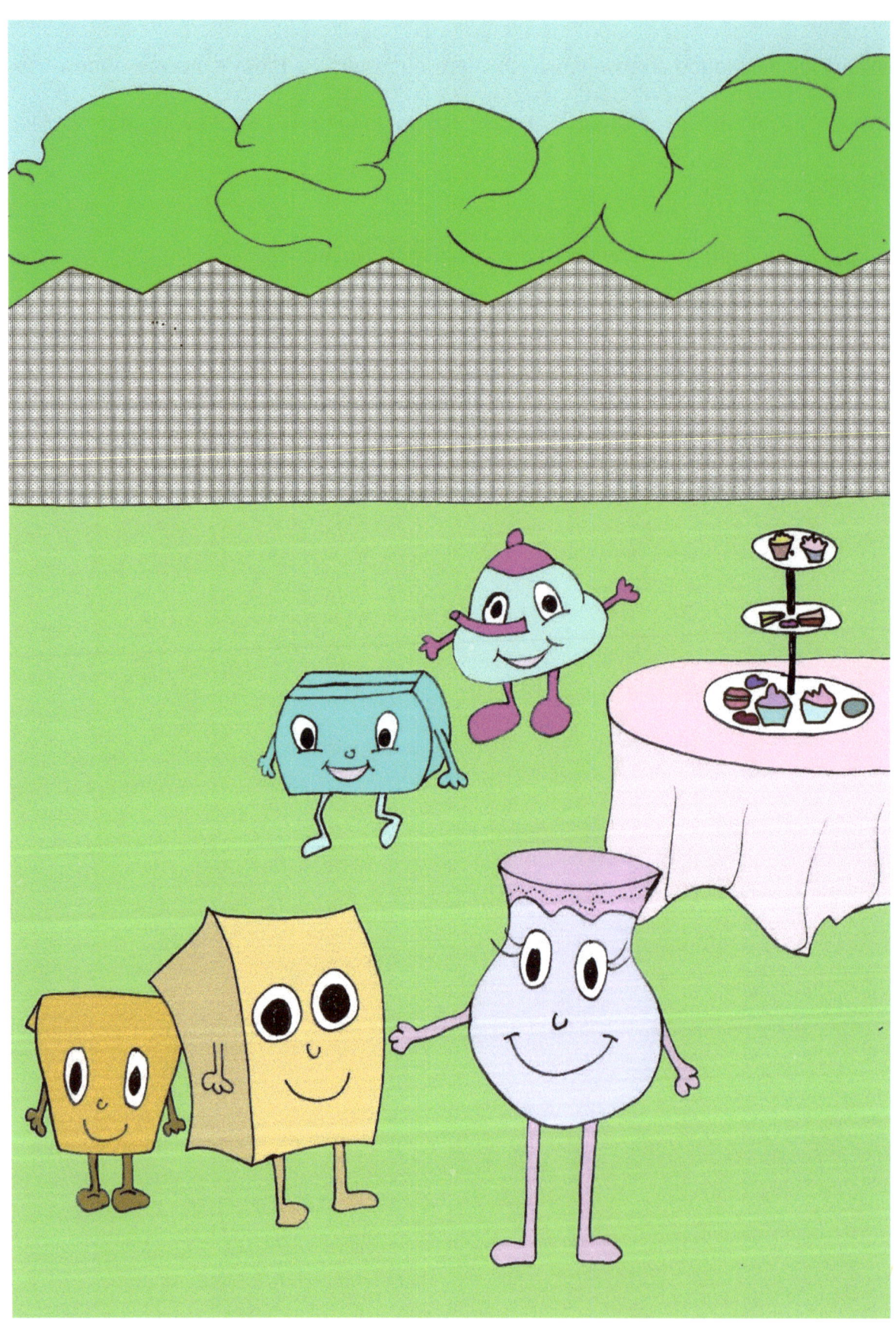

Bibby goes on Holiday

Bibby was deciding where to go on holiday. He thought to himself, 'I'd like to go somewhere I can have the best time ever.'

"Morning Bibby." His friends greeted him.

"Planning on a holiday?" Mr Kettle asked.

"I am yes. I think I'll go to Holiday Land."

"Who with?"

"With all of you of course."

"Hang on a minute we're not taking the holiday car again are we," Toasty asked, "the last time we took that old thing we ended up driving it though the Grumpy Farmer's field, smashing the wall down and letting the sheep loose."

"No, no, no, I've had more driving lessons since then."

The five made a trailer to put everything into. A huge old sheet was tied with rope to cover the things which was to be pulled by the car. When done they set off.

As they got to the edge of the farmer's field he was nowhere to be seen. "Quick open the gates!" Bibby cried out. With a lot of humps and bumps the five made it to the other side.

The next part of their journey was to drive down Long Tree View Road. It was a long straight road with trees either side of it. The hotel was at the bottom. You could also see the beach and the sea behind the hotel. By the time they arrived there was only time to unpack, have a quick look around and then go to bed.

The next day the five could not decide what to do first either go to the beach or the pool. "Let's go to the pool first." Someone suggested. Bibby fetched his lilo for them to use, a beach ball to play with and arm bands for Toasty and Eggcup. They swam and played till the sun went down.

Sunday was the following day and they decided they were going to swim out to Skull Cross Island. Which was a small island off the shore of the beach. No one ever went there because of Pirate Black Shank. It was said that he was the most horrible pirate in the all the lands.

Just before lunch the five began to swim out. Soon, they reached the islands beach. They began to walk on the sand, "Right, let's look for Black Shank's treasure." Bibby suggested. A voice came from behind them.

"Get out of here." The five turned around quickly and began to laugh.

"Please tell me you're not Pirate Black Shank." Bibby chuckled with his hand over his mouth.

"Just because I look like a clown doesn't mean I am not scary. I've spent many years pretending to be a pirate to keep my clown treasure safe."

"Don't worry your secret is safe with us." With that the clown gave the five a gold piece each and sent them on their way.

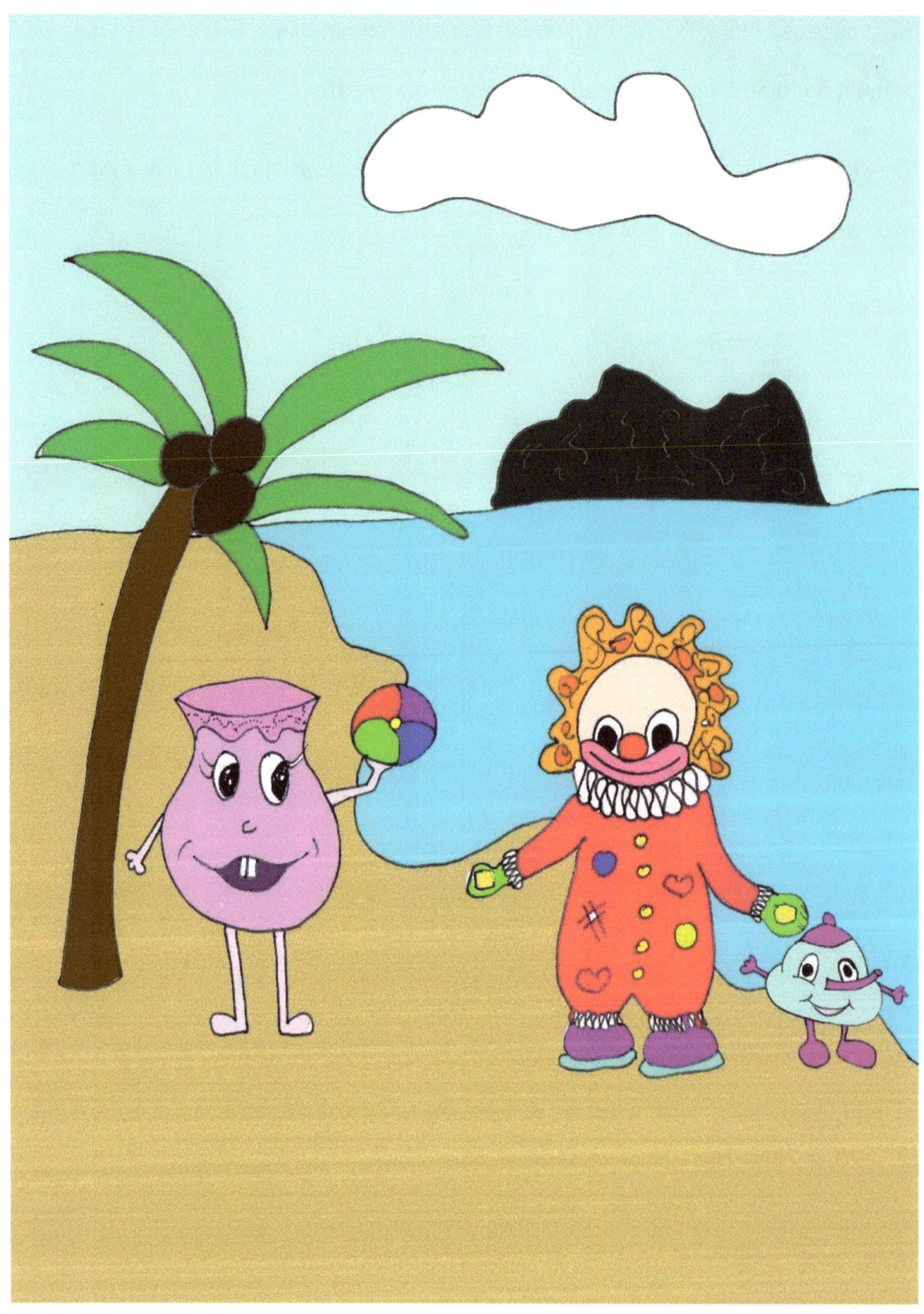

By lunchtime, the five had swam back at the hotel. Evening came, they had packed and were ready for the journey home.

Magic Land

Bibby was learning magic and he was getting quite good. But would his friends be impressed, he decided to invite them round for an evening of tricks.

"Good evening, everybody," his friends put down their drinks, "tonight I am going to perform some magic for you."

"You do magic."

"Watch."

"Have you heard that if you can do magic then you can see Magic Land." Mr Mug replied. They all began to laugh.

"Don't be so silly that was believed many years ago. I've been practising the whole day long and I've not seen any land of that sort." With that Bibby then began to perform the appearing rabbit from inside a top hat trick.

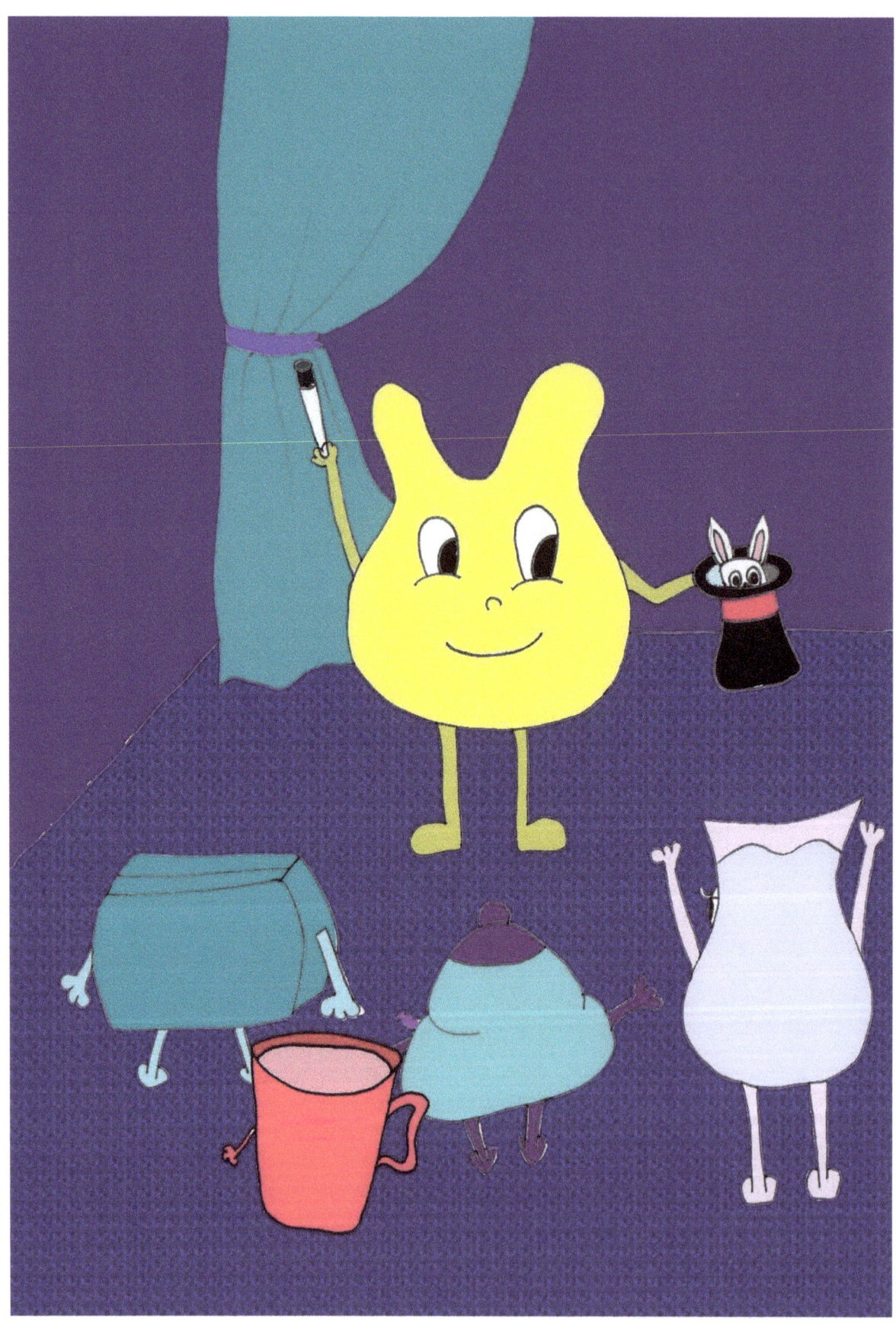

Suddenly, there was a knock at the front door. Bibby went to see who it was. He opened the door. There stood a Wizard. Dressed in white. With a long beard and a magic wand. Thinking that the Wizard was a joke. Bibby decided to let him in. Going along with the fun.

"Do come on in Mr Wizard."

"Thank you. I am also known as the King of Magic Land. If you help me, I will grant you three wishes." As the two walked into where Bibby's friends were. Bibby winked at them. Then looked at what he thought was a stupid Wizard saying, "Yes, of course I will help you."

The King explained that he had lost his way and could not find his home. Without him there soon the land would vanish forever. Bibby suddenly, realised who he was. Straight away he went upstairs pulling out an old chest that had been given to him by his Mum and Dad.

Inside was a big book of spells. He then ran downstairs and gave it to the King. "This may have a spell in it to help you find your way." Looking through the King found nothing.

"Let me have a look." Bibby asked. He started to look through. Coming across a riddle at the back. It read: 'Take the King to the sand to get him back to Magic Land.' Toasty jumped up, "I know there's sand at Holiday Land. The riddle must mean the beach."

"Yes, but there's no Magic Land that I know of there." Eggcup pondered.

"Let's go." Mr Kettle excitedly said.

"How it takes a day to get there." Bibby wondered.

"We'll take my magic carpet." With that they all claimed onto the King's carpet and flew on their way.

When the six arrived sure enough to the right of Skull Cross Island was the King's land. The King was finally home. The people of Magic Land were saved, and Bibby was granted his three wishes as promised.

Can you guess what he wished for? He wished that Town Land would be safe, that all would live happily and that he would be best friends with his four friends forever.

The Small Town Party

"I would like to hold a party here at my house." Bibby announced. Toasty thought it was a great idea and went straight home to get party items.

"What should I do, bake a cake or make some juice?" Eggcup said aloud.

"Do both."

Then the five friends rushed around. Collecting food, baking cakes, and making juice. They were about to sit down and eat when Mr Mug said, "Why don't we barbecue the food?"

"That's a good idea." Eggcup and Toasty excited replied. The five then went to Eggcup's house to set up the barbecue.

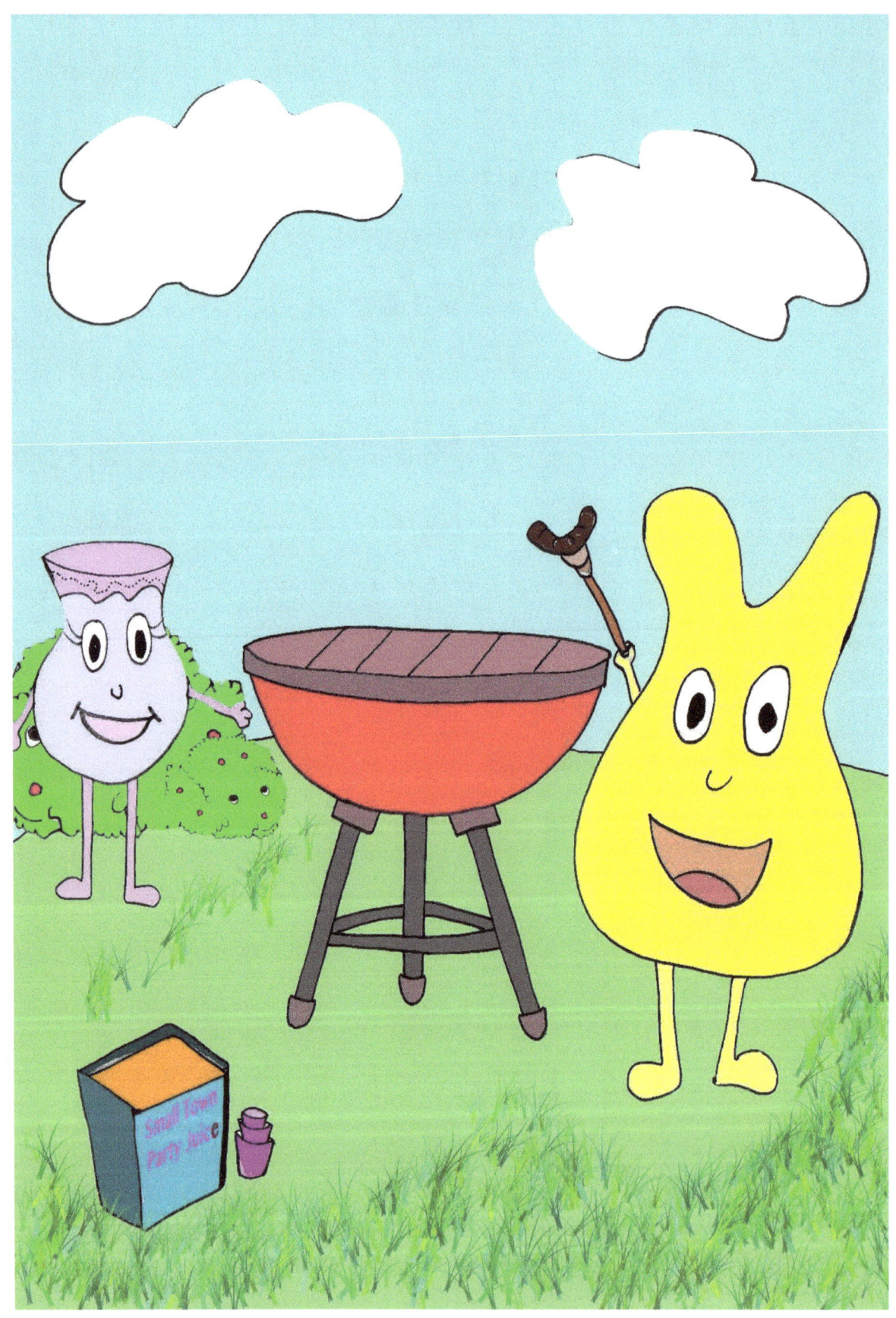

When the barbeque was ready, they cooked and ate all the food. They drank the juice and had some cake. Bibby then put on some music. More juice was made. They then danced, sang, and enjoyed themselves until late into the night.

Recipe for Eggcup's Small-Town Party Juice:

Orange juice

Pineapple juice

Lemonade

The Clock

A clock had appeared in Big Town but where had it come from? Unluckily, it was not quite finished. There were two hands missing. Written on the front of it were the words: 'Town Land Folks Meeting Place.'

Bibby started a search to find out where it had come from and to try to say thank you to whoever had put it there. At the end of the day Bibby had come up with no answers. He went home tired. He took one last look at the clock from his bedroom window and went to bed.

In the morning Bibby woke. Looking out of his window he noticed straight away that one hand of the clock had been placed on the front, 'What on earth?' He thought.

PTO

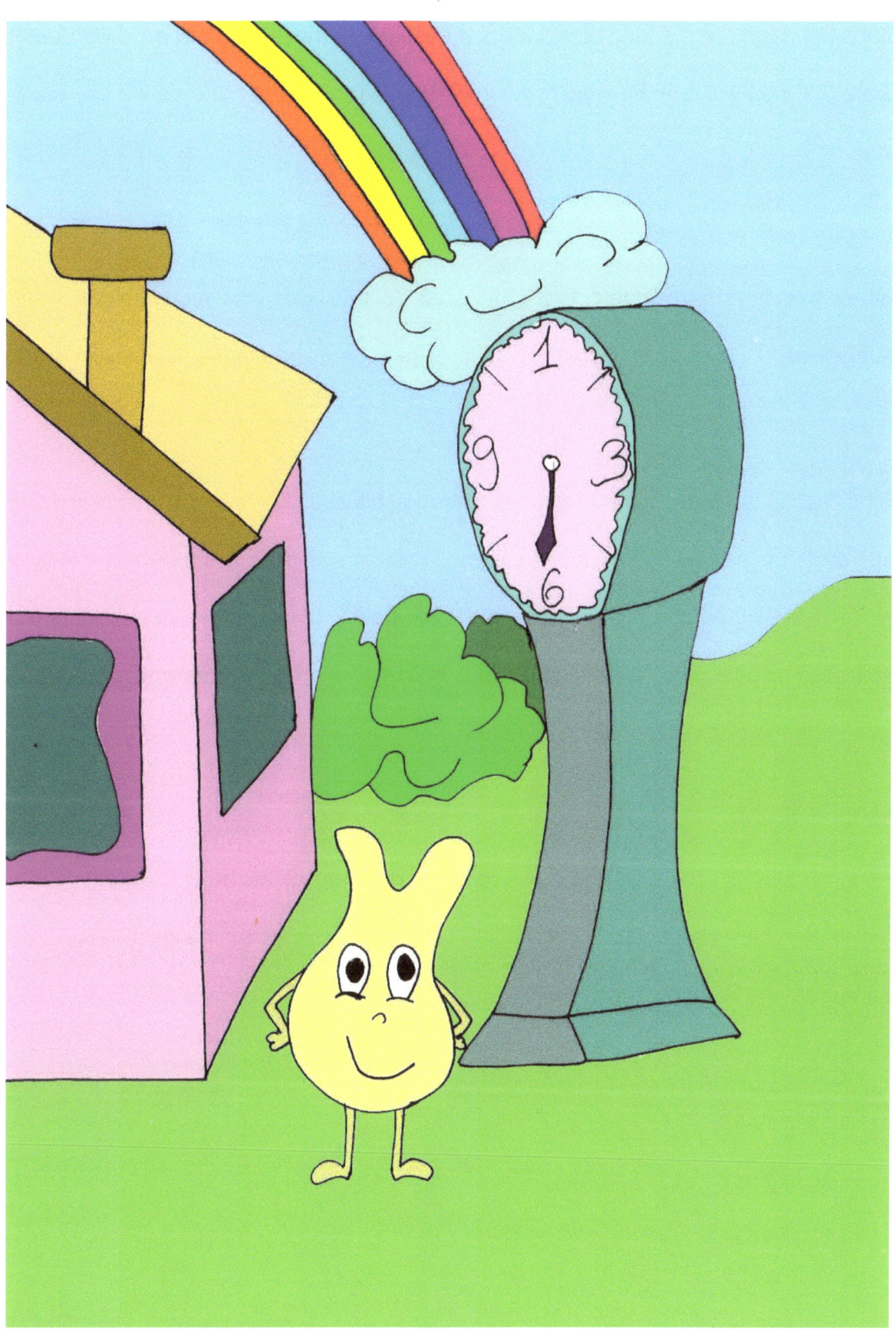

He began the search once more but again found no answers. That evening Bibby called a meeting for Town Land.

Soon, everyone in the land were asking questions, 'Where was it from?' 'Who put it there?' 'When will it be finished?' 'Who will look after it?' and 'Who do we say thank you to?'

Bibby had an idea. He told everyone what he had seen the night before. Then suggested, "I will sit up waiting and hopefully, get some answers to our questions."

Bibby sat up the whole night long looking through his bedroom window. Just before the sun came up, he saw something a rainbow of colours shining from the clock. He looked closely. Seeing people every colour of the rainbow working on the clock. Being too scared to go over Bibby watched from afar. In a blink of an eye whoever they were had gone and the clock was finally complete.

Now, the sun had come up and it was daylight. Bibby shook his head. He went over to the clock. There was a note at the bottom of it: 'This gift is for the people of Town Land from the Rainbow Land People.'

PTO

Bibby was delighted. He went around telling his friends what he had seen and what the letter read. Finally, everyone's questions were answered. It was then decided that Bibby would look after the clock with care forever.

The Circus comes to Town Land

Everybody knows that circuses travel everywhere. One day the circus came to Town Land. Bring loads of rides to play on and stalls to have fun at. It was the biggest circus you have ever seen.

There were clowns to make you laugh, magicians to perform magic, tightrope walkers to walk on the tightrope and fortune tellers to tell your fortune. The circus even had its own bearded lady.

As the circus was unloading Little Mr Mouse shouted, "Get that away from my house!" One of the clowns had dropped a box right at the door of his house.

PTO

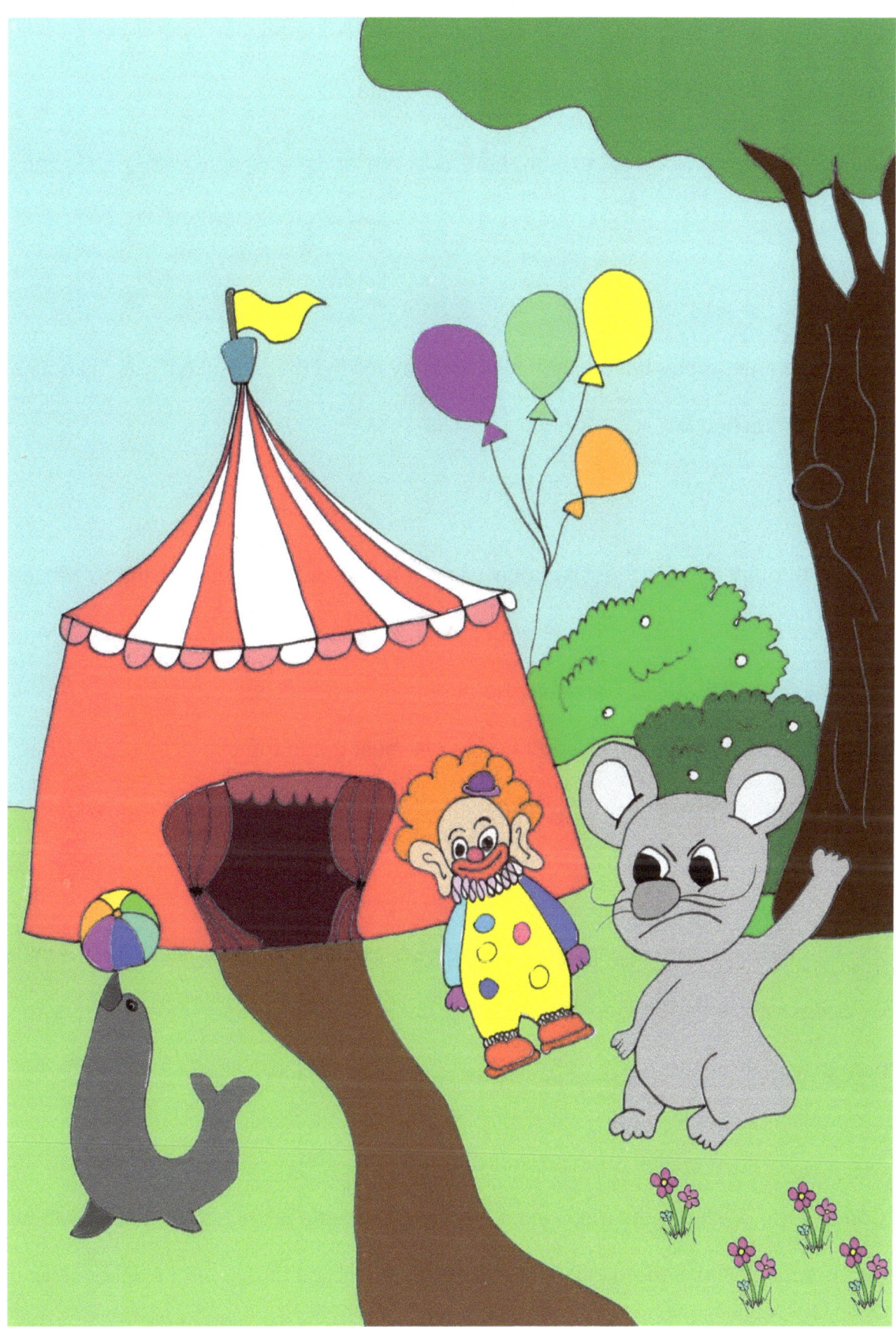

"Right, I've had enough of you lot. If you think you can put up your silly circus near my house, you have got another thing coming." Mr Mouse then went to see Bibby. "Bibby,

Bibby," he was mowing his front lawn, "the circus folk are banging and making loads of noise. It's driving me mad we've got to make it go."

"You've got two choices either stay here with me or go and stay with the Grumpy Farmer?"

After some time, Bibby had calmed him down by talking him into staying at his house until the circus had left.

Looking through Bibby's guest bedroom window the following morning. Little Mr Mouse could see most Town Land members already at the circus playing on the rides and having fun on the stalls. Suddenly, he changed his mind about the circus he now wanted to go and have fun there. "Quickly, we must get to the circus." They washed, dressed, and went over.

Arriving everyone was waiting to go into a big yellow and red Circus Marquee. As they got closer people had started to go in. They could also see a man at the front waving them over.

"Come on in." Invitingly the man said. They went in. Inside the marquee there could be seen the magicians performing, tight rope walkers walking ropes, fortune tellers telling people their fortune and clowns doing funny things. Even the bearded lady could be seen stroking her beard.

When the show was over Town Land spent the rest of the day playing, having fun on the rides and stalls. "Can I stay at your house again?" Little Mr Mouse asked. Bibby agreed. That night the two talked and talked about the wonderful day they had.

The next day Mr Mouse awoke and looked out of Bibby's Guest Bedroom window once more. The circus was packed and nearly ready to go. In a flash he was dressed and had ran across to the clown that he had shouted at the day before.

"Mr Clown I would like to thank you for a lovely day yesterday and I am sorry for snapping at you. After all even clowns can make mistakes."

"Thank you." The Clown replied and with that the circus was gone.

Water Park Fun

Bibby decided to go to the water park with his friends. They all decided that a good time to go would be on a quiet day because there would be hardly anyone around. They then could do pretty much what they wanted.

Unlike going to the Fair which was right near to the Grumpy Farmers Farm in Big Town. The park was near to Reverend Robinson's Church.

The friends wondered how to get the speed boat and the wind surf boards to the park. So, Bibby had to borrow the holiday car from his parents. The five packed and began their journey.

When the five arrived at the park Bibby and Mr Mug jumped out of the car diving straight into the water. Meanwhile Mr Kettle, Eggcup and Toasty put the boat and the boards onto the water's edge.

After swimming for some time Bibby and Mr Mug put the boat in the water and climbed in. "Come on," Bibby suggested to the others, "let us go for a search around." The five decided to take the boat round the park to every place they could.

The park was not very, big. Soon, the five had finished the trip of the park's ponds and rivers. However, they had come to a sign. It had written on it in big letters, 'KEEP OUT!'

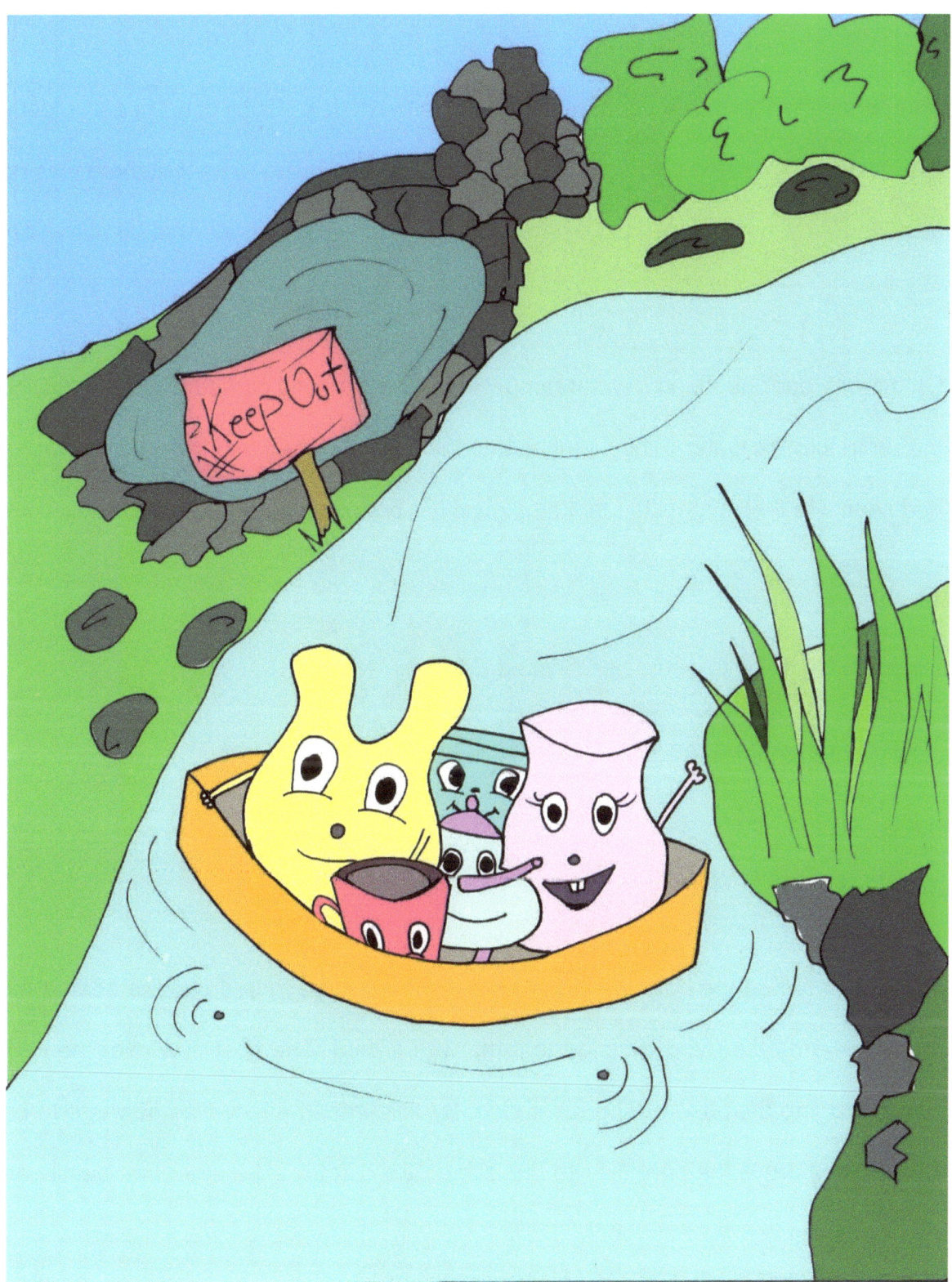

Bibby and the others decided to pull up the sign and go through. The grass either side of the river was long, and they could see nothing but the river ahead of them. Driving through they came to a dead end. Bibby decided to see if there was anything on the other side.

Sure, enough there was a pond with an island in the middle. Bibby could see an elderly lady hanging out some clothes on her washing line. He called to her but there was no answer. Bibby then decided to go back to the boat to tell the others what he had seen.

On his way back he found a water ramp. He picked it up and carried it back. Throwing the ramp into the water, Bibby jumped into the boat and then told the others what he had seen. He then suggested that they go in the boat to try and reach the lady.

"How are we going to get to her?" Asked Eggcup.

"With the ramp of course."

"I hope it's safe."

Bibby then turned the boat around. Reversing it back. He then drove the boat at full speed towards the ramp. Hitting the ramp with a thud. The boat flew over the long grass and into the pond on the other side. By this time, the lady was nowhere to be seen. Bibby drove the boat over to the island. "Be careful." The other four cautioned him as he climbed from the boat.

"Bibby," called Mr Kettle, "there's a witch in these parts somewhere."

"Please stop worrying I'll be fine."

Bibby then knocked the door of the lady's house. The door opened, the lady came out and looked him up and down. Telling him, "I am a witch. But luckily for you little one I am a nice witch. There is a witch who lives on the next island who is not so nice. So, be careful."

"Why are you here in the middle of nowhere?" Bibby questioned.

The witch then told Bibby that the reason she was there was to warn people of the Wicked Witch of the Lands that lived in the next pond. Climbing back into the boat the five headed for the safety of the main park.

They then spent the rest of the day wind surfing.

The Return of the Good Guys

There was an unusual event that took place called, 'The Four Shooting Stars.' This is where four stars fly through the sky at the same time. All were to see this happening.

Unknown to Captain Colson and her superheroes, Darton had hidden a magic spell. On a scroll in a box under the stables. Whilst he was cleaning out the stables one day he remembered where it was.

Darton knew that if he were to read out the spell whilst hiding behind the Old Oak Tree as the stars flew by, he and his gang would get their powers back. This by the way would allow Darton and his gang to have another try at destroying Town Land.

Meanwhile Town Land rushed around getting food, drink, and music ready for the evening ahead. That night they gathered at the top of Little Mr Mouse's home by the tree. Music was switched on and soon the party was in full swing. "Quickly we must hide. The stars will be coming over soon." Darton ordered.

The shooting stars began to fly over. Darton started to read the spell, "Zigaty, Zigaty, Zand, gives us the powers to destroy Town Land." The stars then joined into one.

The land looked on not knowing what was happening. A now one bright star let out a beam of light right behind the tree. The spell had worked. Darton and his gang had their powers back.

Soon, Darton and his gang were back at their base at the farm cooking up a plan, "Now I am Dastardly Darton Dark once more I will destroy this land forever."

Meanwhile Mrs Colson and her fellows had left the park and had changed into their superhero disguises, "Find Dastardly and his men. Tell me what they are up to because the happening was quite different this evening." Captain Colson told Chester the Chocolate Labrador.

Chester then ran as fast as his legs could carry him to the base where the bad guys were. By this time, the bad guys plan was already in action.

A T-Rex dinosaur was in the horses, stables making an awful noise. Roaring and roaring louder than a wild lion. Chester howled to signal the rest of the gang to come quick. When they had arrived the T-Rex had already been released.

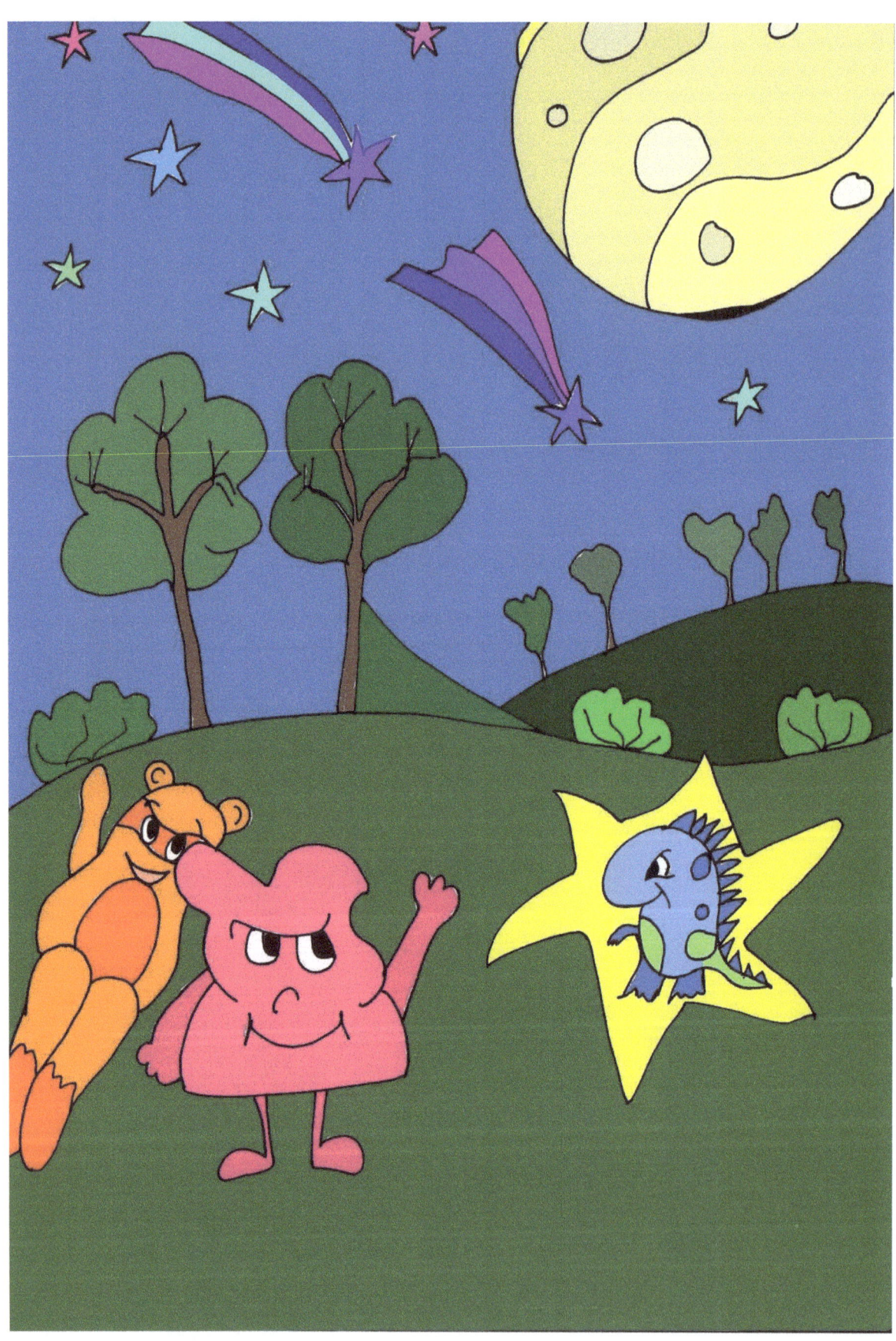

The T-Rex was the most terrifying dinosaur you have ever seen. Dastardly had used his gang's powers to bring him from the past and he was very hungry. "We have to act fast," shouted Captain Colson, "get some rope." She ordered.

"I have rope." Cape Crusader Kirby answered.

"Tie him down." After a lot of hard work, the T-Rex was tied down safely and was sent back to his home. Town Land was saved once more.

Bibby's Lazy Day

It was Saturday and Bibby had decided to do nothing. "Bibby," Mr Kettle asked, "are you coming to the Big Town Fair today?"

"No thank you I'm doing nothing all day."

The four friends looked at each other and said, "Oh well, we'll leave him here." They then set off for the Fair.

When they arrived, they began enjoying the fair as usual but soon it was evening and nearly closing time. Mr and Mrs Bib invited everybody to their house for supper, "Shall we invite Bibby?"

"Yes of course." Mr Mug replied.

Off they went to his house. They arrived only to find that the curtains were drawn. "Bibby!" They shouted. Bibby jumping fell out bed. "Supper is at your Mum and Dad's house are you coming?"

"No thank you I'm nothing all day."

They looked at each other, "Oh well, we'll leave him here." They then set off to eat. After they had gone Bibby decided that he would make himself a sandwich. As he was now awake and hungry. Once he had eaten, he cleared up. Then jumped straight back into bed.

Over at his parent's house the meal was delicious. After they had finished eating, Toasty suggested, "Why don't we see if Bibby wants to join us for dessert?"

"What a great idea."

Soon, everyone from Town Land were outside Bibby's house once more. By this time, he was fast asleep yet again. "Bibby." He awoke sharply.

Getting up. Opening his upstairs curtains and window. Leaning out said, "Can't a Bib get any sleep around here."

"Would you like to join us for pudd?"

"No thank you I'm doing nothing all day." With that he slammed the window, shut the curtains, and climbed back into bed.

They did not know what to do, "I think Bibby should make friends with the Grumpy Farmer." Someone suggested the rest agreed.

Then Mr Kettle had an idea, "Let's go to the park for a while and then try later." They tried and tried. But every time they got the same answer.

"No thank you I'm doing nothing all day."

By late evening Bibby finally got out of bed. Washed. Dressed and opened his front door. Only to find the rest of Town Land on the other side. "My word," He, said startled, "now I am up would anyone like to skim stones down at the Big Pond for the evening?" By this time, it was getting late and everyone was tired. Little Mr Mouse grumbled, "No way I going to the pond. You are the laziest Bib I have ever met. I am going home to bed. Good night."

Bibby looked surprised, "Would anyone else?"

"No thank you." They said leaving Bibby stood at his doorstep.

PTO

Bibby feeling very lazy, silly, and awake spent the rest of the evening alone skimming stones down at the Big Pond.

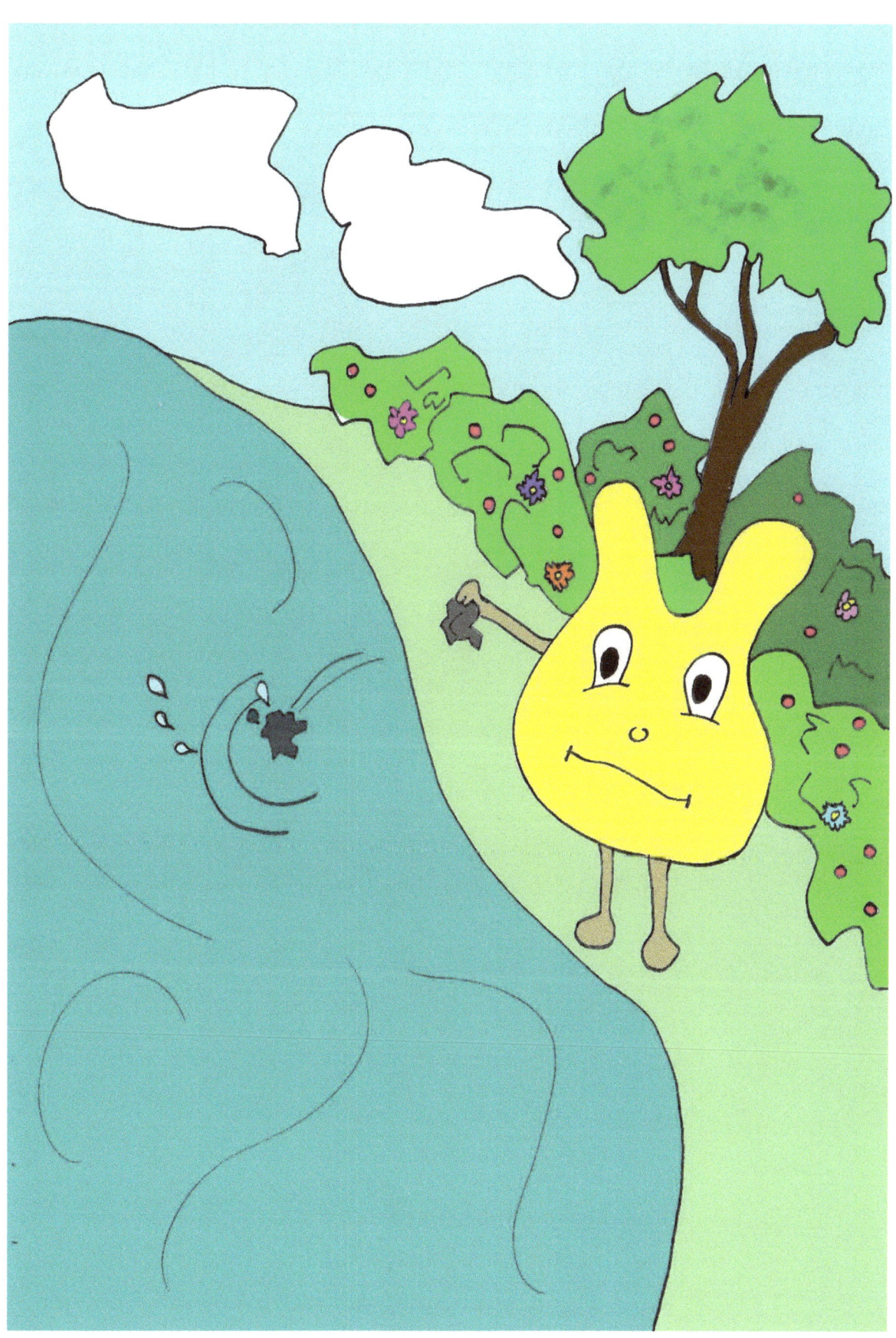

The Town Land Zoo

The zoo was run by the Zoo People who did a particularly good job. They were very, clean and caring. It was nearly that time of year again for Town Land to start visiting. There was going to be a Royal opening. The King of Magic Land was the VIP guest.

It was the night before the opening and the Zookeeper thought it would be a good idea to let the animals out of their houses for a little walk at the same time. The animals were allowed out for walks every day but never together. Before long, the animals started to argue about their homes. "Come on now please it's the opening tomorrow."

"We will not go back to our house until it's like the monkey's." The elephants said.

"We want more room, so we want the lion's house." The snakes moaned.

The Keeper not knowing what to do went to see Bibby. "Bibby, Bibby, help me please."

"Go away I'm asleep."

"Please Bibby please." Bibby threw off the bed covers, put on his dressing gown and slippers, and went to see what the problem was.

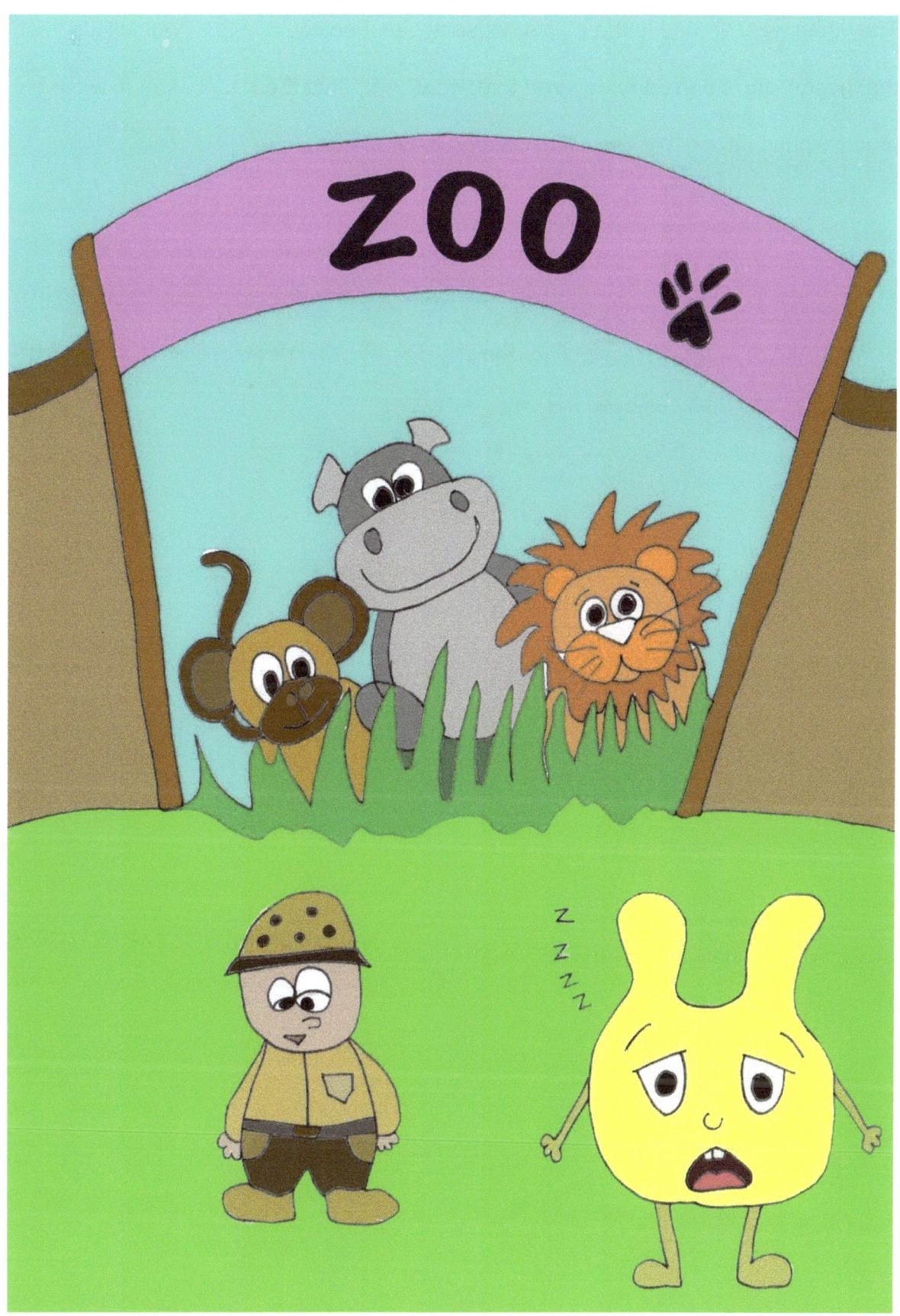

The Keeper explained everything to him. Bibby replied, "This may need the help of the King."

They then went around to the King's house to see if he could help, "I would love to so that everything is perfect for my visit tomorrow." With that the King began to wave his magic wound saying, "Animals that rage go back to your cage."

When Bibby and the Keeper returned to the zoo. Luckily, the animals were peacefully in their homes fast asleep. The next day arrived and everyone except for a very tired Zookeeper and Bibby enjoyed the day.

Bob and Sam's Special Day

It was nearly the twins, birthday. "Good morning Toasty," Bob and Sam proudly said as he walked into the Big Town Post Office.

"Morning. I've only popped up for some stamps."

"We're having a party in two weeks it's our birthdays. Would you like to come with your friends?"

"Yes, we'd love to."

Toasty then set off on his way to tell his friends about the birthday. Bibby as always was not happy and just had to add his bit, "We must organize a surprise party for them."

"How on earth are we going to do that if they are having a party at theirs," Toasty asked, "if we have a party here and no one goes to theirs they will think that no one likes them."

"What I will do is phone them both sometime before and ask them to come over for some tea," Bibby cleverly said. As he then set about giving his friends jobs to do for the surprise party.

Toasty was given the task of making the party food, Eggcup had to be a party clown,

Mr Kettle was in charge of the party games (musical chairs and pass the parcel), Mr Mug was to make cake and get a bouncy castle. Whilst Bibby organised music and the others to come from every town and land.

Some days went by and on the day of the party as arranged at Bibby's house everyone arrived. Bibby told them to be quiet. Picking up his phone. He then invited Bob and Sam over for a cup of tea. Both agreed and set off on their way to his house. "It's very quiet in Town Land today everyone must be getting ready to come to our party?" Bob mentioned to Sam.

Soon, they arrived at Bibby's house. They knocked on the front door. As the door opened everyone shouted, "Surprise." The two were delighted.

Eggcup came out dressed as a clown and began to tell jokes. The two games were played and were a hit. They played music and ate cake. The bouncy castle was used, and all were happy the whole day long.

PTO

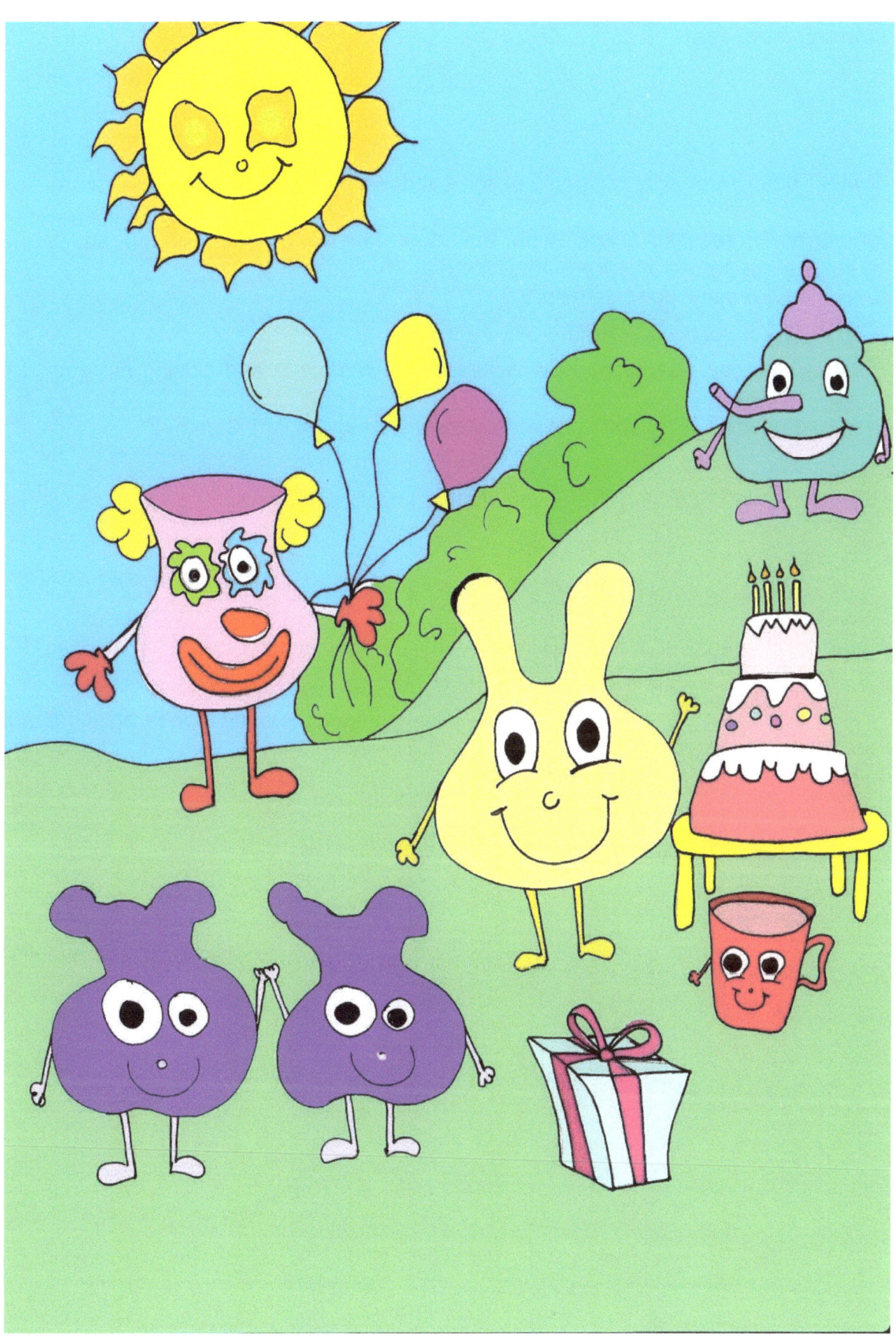

Jammy, Jam, Jam

Sweet Tooth Sarah was hungry. So, she sat down and began to wonder what to have for dinner. There was a knock on her front door. She went over to the door and opened it, "Harwo," Jammy, Jam, Jam said.

"Evening Jammy," Sarah happily replied letting Jammy in and closing the door. She then had an idea, "Can you cook me some of your lovely jam, Jammy?"

"Why certainly." Suddenly there was another knock at the door.

Sarah went to answer it. It was Silly Cereal. "Are you eating because I'm starving?"

"Yes, I am. Jammy has come over and he is going to help me. We're having jam on toast."

"That's great I can put the jam on some cereal." That was Silly Cereal's favourite.

PTO

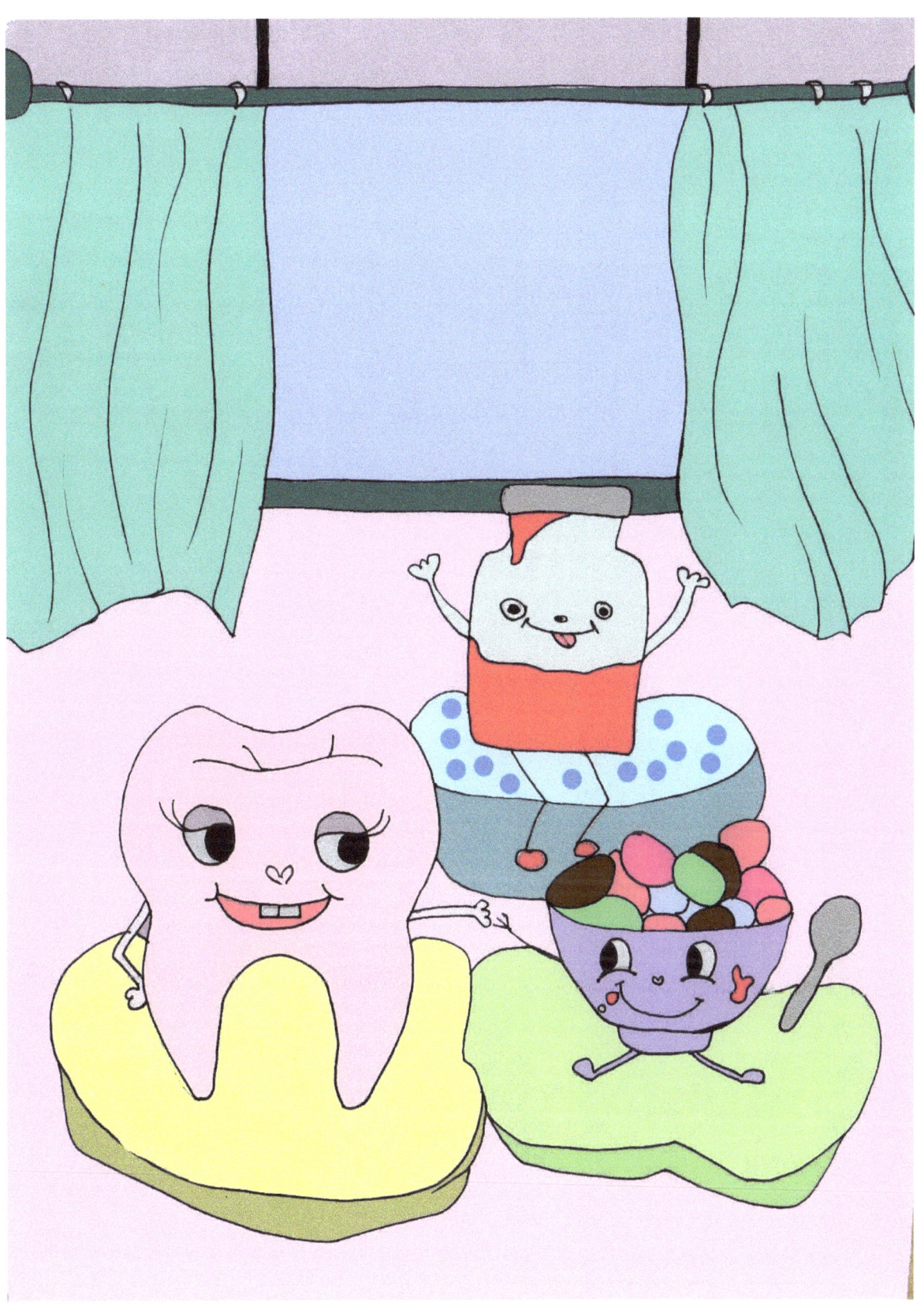

After time, the now homemade jam was ready. The three sat down to eat. They ate and ate and ate, till their tummies were full. "Shall we have a sleep over as well?" Sarah questioned.

"I'd love to. I am so full up. I don't think I could walk home anyway." Silly Cereal replied. Sarah then set up the beds in the lounge, with that Jammy, Jam, Jam decided to go home. After he had left the other two were so tired, they both went straight to bed.

Soon it was morning. Sweet Tooth Sarah was slowly waking up. Silly Cereal was still asleep. 'Aw,' Sarah thought to herself ignoring the pain she had. She then made some toast for breakfast. Using the leftover jam from the night before.

"Aw." Silly Cereal screamed in pain as she awoke. She then went to the kitchen to look for her friend. As she walked into the kitchen Sarah was just about to take a bite of her toast. "Aw," Sarah cried out, "my tooth is saw."

"And mine."

"What are we to do?"

"I think it's time for a trip to see Dolly the Dentist." Silly Cereal said. The two then set off to Dolly's Dentist.

"Please help us." They both asked as they arrived.

"Off course I can," Dolly said as she sat them both in her dentist chairs, "looks like you've eaten too many sweets. I'll have to put a filling in."

"What!?"

Dolly then began to fit their fillings. Luckily before long Sweet Tooth Sarah and Silly Cereal's teeth were fixed. "What have you both been eating?" Dolly asked.

"Jam." They both replied.

"Try not to eat so much next time." The two were pleased that their pain had gone. Then they got up out of the chairs and went home and had salad for dinner.

Jumble, Jumble

"Mr Kettle," Bibby said, "would you be so kind as to help me tidy out my spare room?" Mr Kettle agreed and they both set about tidying. As they were doing so Bibby found some old photos.

Looking through the pictures made Bibby remember. "Bibby are you, all right?"

"I'm okay. I just found these pictures. Do you remember the day in this picture?" Bibby then passed over a photograph.

"Yes, I do." The two then began to sit pondering the fun that they had on that day.

The pictures reminded them both of when they went go-carting. As they thought back looking at the pictures they laughed and laughed together. "Come Bibby. We must carry on and finish tidying out your room."

When the two finished they looked at the things to be thrown out, "Why don't we have a jumble sale Bibby?"

"What a good idea."

PTO

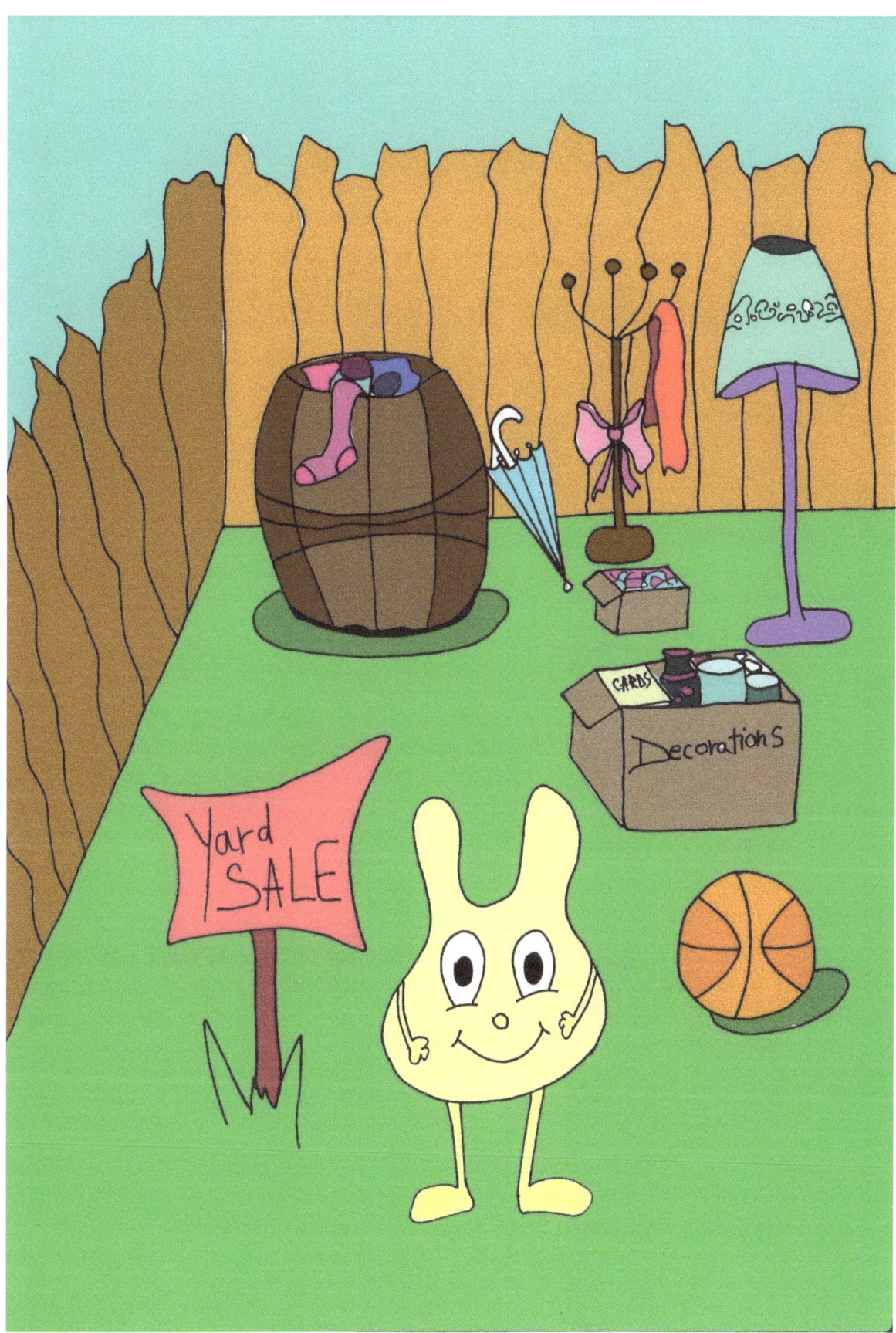

The next day at first no one turned up. "I've thought of an idea to get people here."

Bibby said.

"What's that?"

"I will sing a sales song. Roll up! Roll up! Jumble, jumble got to go, low, low prices don't say no."

Slowly but surely people from all over Town Land started to arrive. In time Bibby's old belongings were gone and soon people were starting to get tired.

Before they knew it, the day was over.

Bibby goes to Market

It was market day. There was a stall for everything that you could think of. Clothing, games, meat, fish and even aftershave and perfume stalls.

There was also to be a band. This was organized by the Reverend Robinson and was to be held at the Big Town Church. It was early. The market could be seen setting up. Slowly but surely the stalls were prepared and the items for sale were put out.

"Are you up Bibby," Toasty asked, "time to go to the market."

"Oh yes it's today. Just coming."

In no time Bibby and Toasty gathered the members of Town Land. They set off. When arriving they split up and looked at the different things.

PTO

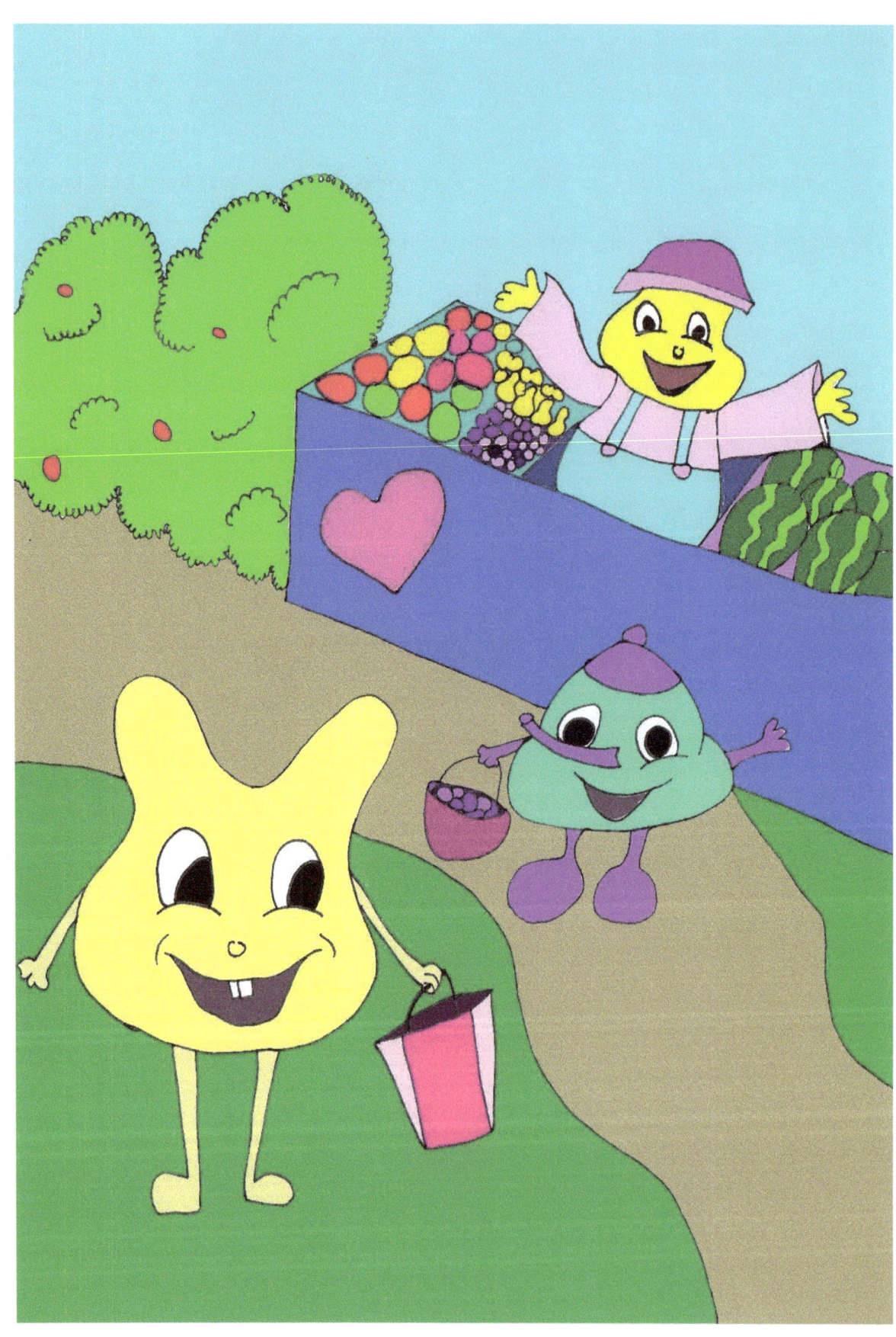

Time went by and at the end of the day Tommie asked Bibby, "What have you bought from the market?"

"I have bought three games and a bird's nest for Little Mr Mouse." With that Bibby handed the gifts to Mr Mouse.

Everyone then headed home with their shopping to get ready for the band that evening. Whilst the band was setting up the market people quickly packed everything away and left.

On the way home Little Mr Mouse began to think, "Where can I put this bird's nest to attract the birds and what on earth am, I going to do with these games?"

When he had arrived at his house at the park. He thought to himself, 'Right I'll put the bird's nest in the Old Oak Tree and the games I will use every time someone comes to visit.'

Soon, it was time for the band to begin. The Reverend Robinson had run around to everybody telling them where to meet. As he had forgotten to hand out the tickets earlier that day. Incidentally, the band was brilliant, and all enjoyed their music.

The following morning Little Mr Mouse awoke to the sound of a bird singing. As he lay in his bed, he suddenly realized it was coming from the nest.

He got out of bed quietly and looked through his front door. Sure, enough there was a bird happily singing away.

He decided to call him Mr Bird and they became the best of friends forever.

Tug of War

The Reverend Robinson had put up a list of two teams. It was going to be Small Town, the Town Land Park and those from the Grumpy Farmer's Farm versus everyone else in Big Town who wanted to join in. The Reverend was to referee.

In case you may have forgotten Small Town has Bibby, Mr Kettle, Toasty, Eggcup and Mr Mug. The Town Land Park has Little Mr Mouse, Mr Worm and Mr Bird living there. At the Farm live the Grumpy Farmer, Fred, Rita, Darton and Teddy.

The rest of Big Town who wanted to take part were Mrs Colson, Jacob, Kirby, and Chester the Labrador from the Big Town Fair. Also, Mr and Mrs Bib from the Big Town Fish and Chip Shop, Parcel, and Tommie the parcels. Bob and Sam from the Big Town Post Office.

"It seems like it's going to be a fair match then Mrs Colson." The Reverend declared. Bibby was not pleased because he had been put on the same team as the Grumpy Farmer.

Bibby had also noticed that there were thirteen people on one team and ten on the other. He offered to go and get a few special friends of his to help, out.

On returning with the King of Magic Land and the Pirate Black Shank from Skull Cross Island he then invited the Reverend Robinson to join in.

"Shall we get started? On your marks and after three…tug!" The teams began to tug as hard as they could.

"Pull!" shouted Bibby's team.

"Heave!" Called out the Reverend's team. The rope went backwards and forwards side to side.

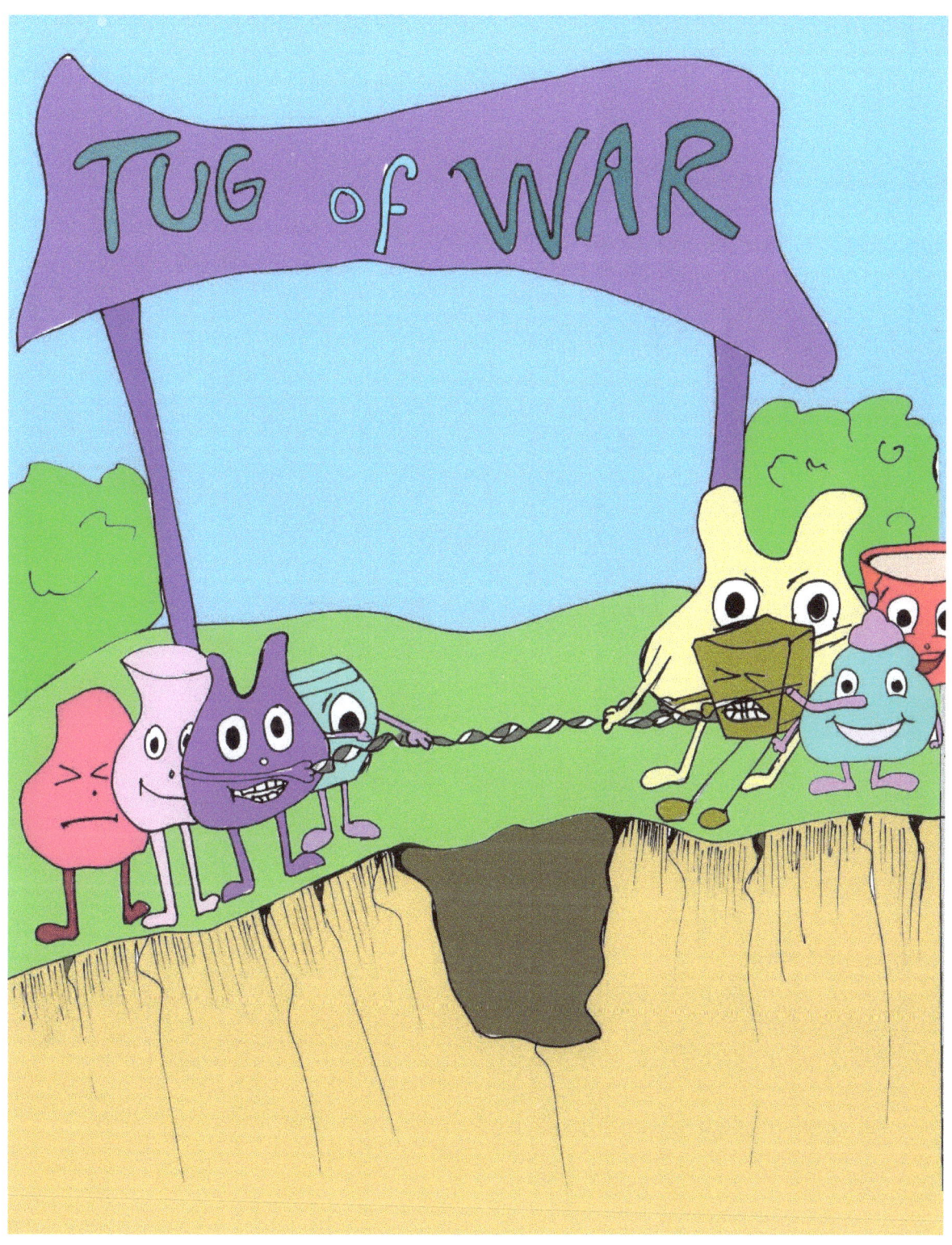

With a massive twang the rope snapped. Both teams fell flat on their backs rolling around in fits of laughter. The tug of war was declared a draw.

Home Help

It was early morning and Twice a Day Ted went to get some ice-cream from Bibby's shop. He always went there twice a day. "Morning Bibby."

PTO

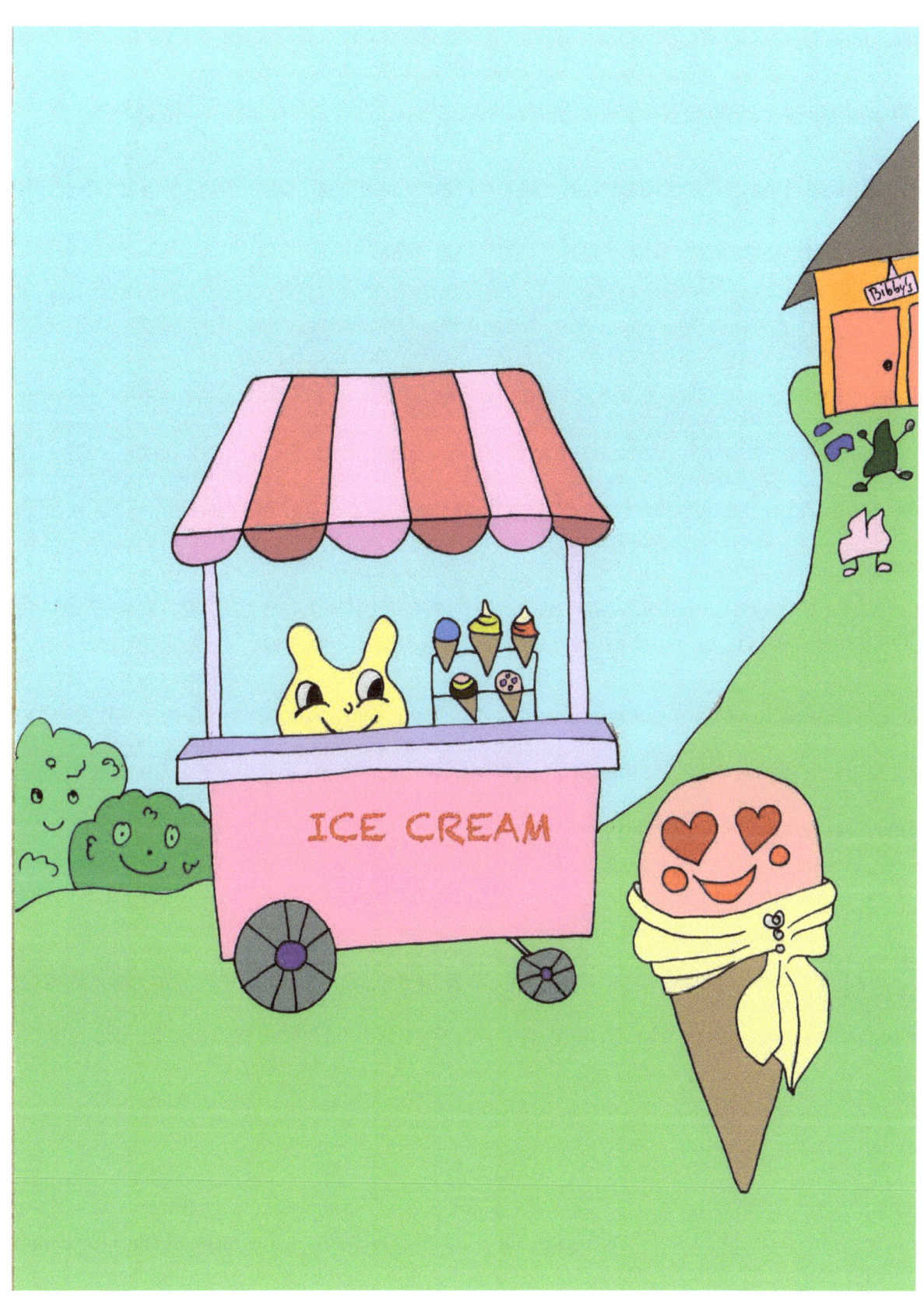

"Morning."

"I have come for my first helping of ice-cream. Have you got walnut whip please?"

"Of course, I have." Bibby served the ice cream and then sat down for a chat as they usually did.

Unknown to Bibby Side-line Sam was setting up shop at Bibby's house for everyone without his permission. Back over at the ice-cream shop. Bibby and Twice a Day Ted were having a really good time. "Bibby what are you doing after severing here at the shop?"

"I'm thinking of going home and having a lovely afternoon nap."

"I don't know how I am going to pay for my second helping today, Bibby. Maybe I will have to do some work for the Grumpy Farmer, thank you anyway?" With that Twice a Day Ted finished his serving and left.

Bibby then tidied up and shut shop. Heading home he felt tired. He stopped at the Big Pond for a nap. It was a lovely day as it usually was in Town Land and before long, he fell fast asleep.

Meanwhile over in Small Town. Side-line Sam was having the time of his life. Selling his belongings, "Stop, stop, stay here and shop," he sang.

Bibby woke up. He, set off for home. He arrived only to find that his house had all of Town Land in it. "My word! What are you all doing here?"

Side-line Sam quickly started to pack away his stuff. Bibby looked annoyed, "What do you think you are doing?"

"Me, nothing." Everyone in Town Land soon realised what Side-line Sam had done and quickly disappeared. Side-line Sam's remaining stuff was everywhere. Bibby was really, angry. "I needed somewhere to sell my things," Sam collie said, "I won't do it again."

Bibby then had an idea he decided to phone Twice a Day Ted. Remembering that he needed money for a second helping of ice-cream.

"Fancy earning your next portion of ice-cream Ted?"

"That would be great."

Twice a Day Ted was delighted, and he headed straight over to Bibby's house. Before long Side-line Sam's things were packed away and Bibby was happy once more.

Soldiers Come to Town

The people were preparing for the day when the Town Land Soldiers came. This event was something that all enjoyed. The soldiers were coming the next day and Bibby's parents were at home making plans for them, "Should we get a chef you think?"

As they were speaking Bibby walked into the dining room. "I'll do the cooking with my friends. I will go straight round and tell them now. Bye Mum, bye Dad." With that Bibby ran off without giving them a chance to speak.

"Friends guess what we are going to cook for the soldiers tomorrow."

"What are we going to cook for them?" Eggcup questioned. "I know what they'd love, spaghetti bolognaise."

"What a good idea Eggcup."

"Right then we'll meet tomorrow and go to the shop to get everything."

The next day arrived and the five friends went around to the Big Town Shop. "Afternoon you lot. What mischief are you getting up to today then?" questioned Granny Bib. Bibby told his Gran, "We have offered to cook today so we're here to get mince, spaghetti and bolognaise sauce."

"Here you are then everything you will need. Oh yes, and some parmesan cheese to go on top. Good luck." Granny and Granddad Bib kindly said after taking time to pick them the stock they had from the back of the shop.

The five arrived back at Bibby's house and began. When the mince and spaghetti were ready Bibby suggested, "Shall we put the spaghetti to drain and leave the mince on one side. Then heat the bolognaise sauce. When the sauce is cooked, we can serve the dinner with the bolognaise in the middle and the spaghetti around the outside."

The other four also had different ideas of how to serve the dinner. After a while, a food fight broke out. They began throwing the bolognaise sauce at each other. Then the mince. Then the spaghetti was thrown. Mr Kettle sided with Eggcup and he began to grate the cheese as Eggcup threw it at Bibby, Toasty and Mr Mug.

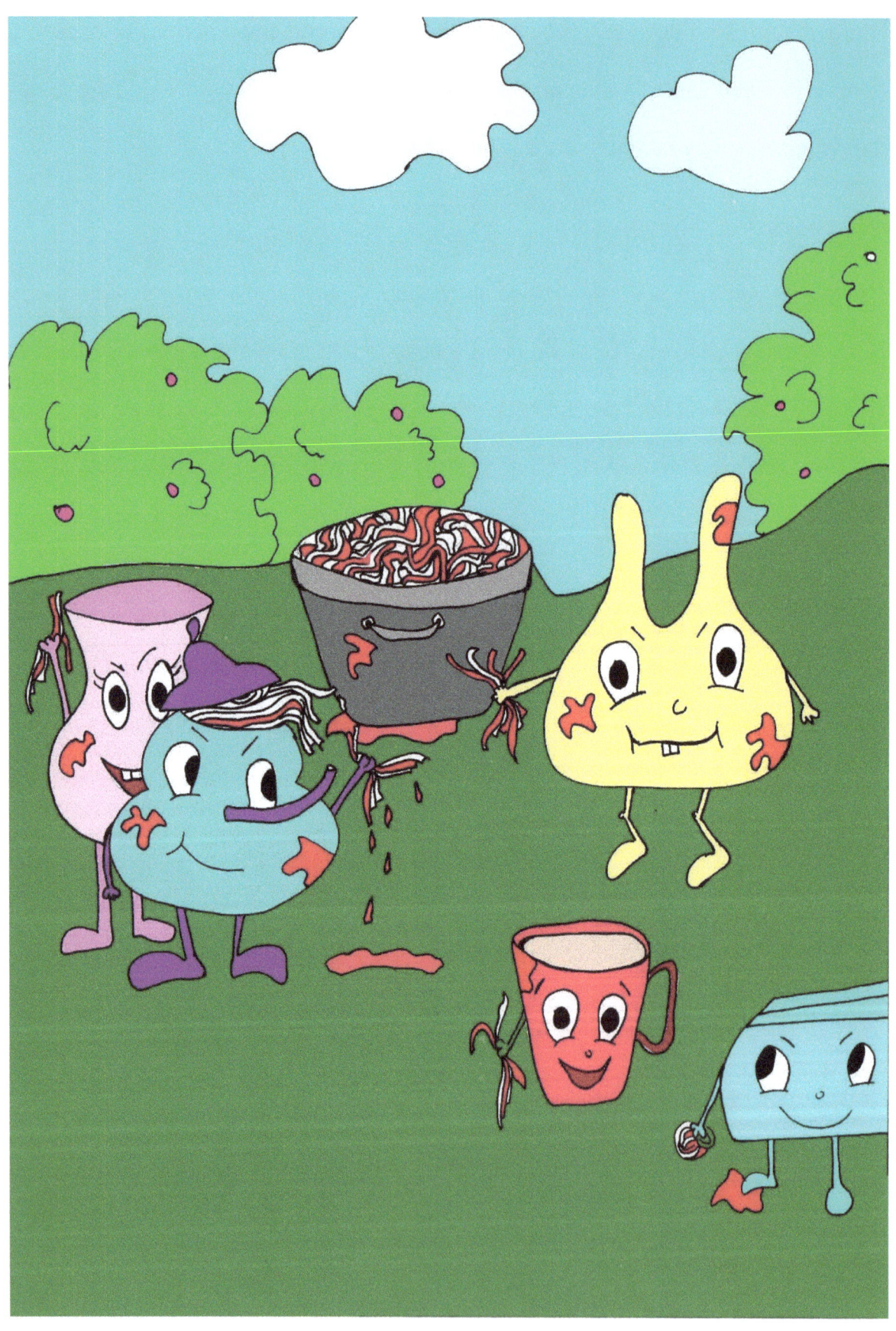

"Stop that!" Bibby's Mum shouted, "Clean up this mess right now." The five began to clean up. "It's a good job Mr Bib and I did not trust you lot from the start. Luckily, we had kept back the best ingredients. When you have cleaned up, I will supervise you cooking the soldier's dinner properly."

By dinner time the soldiers had arrived. Thanks to Mrs Bib the meal was cooked and ready to be served on time. Bibby and his four friends served the meal. After all they had been so very naughty earlier that day.

White Cloud Wonder

Bob and Sam where at the Big Pond waiting for the Train Man. The sun was out shining down on the two as they waited. Today was a special day because the Train Man was going to put on a new show. The Train Land people had made the train so that it would make shapes when blowing smoke out of its chimney.

"Do you think he will turn up?" Bob said to Sam.

"He should do?"

"It's 10am where is he?" Suddenly, there was a clang, a bang, a chuff, a choo and a stop too. The Train Man had arrived.

"You're here!"

"Good morning what a day it is."

"Yes lovely," Bob agreed, "are you ready for the Big Town chimney day?"

"Well, the thing is the train's broken. My people, the Train Land folk and I have been trying to fix it."

Bob and Sam looked shocked. "What are we to do?"

"I know," Sam said, "have you tried cleaning the train?"

"That's right. Little Mr Mouse can help us." Bob chuntered.

Bob and Sam jumped onto the train. Then they headed over to the Town Land Park. "Mr Mouse, Mr Mouse, can you help the Train Man?"

Little Mr Mouse knew exactly what to do. He got out of his cleaning equipment, made a pile with some old firewood from his log fire the night before and began to get to work. In no time at the train was spotless and was piled high with firewood.

The Train Man started to put the wood onto the fire underneath the chimney. He then pressed the 'Wood Lighting Button' and soon the train started to smoke. "We're up and running. The White Cloud Day will still go ahead."

PTO

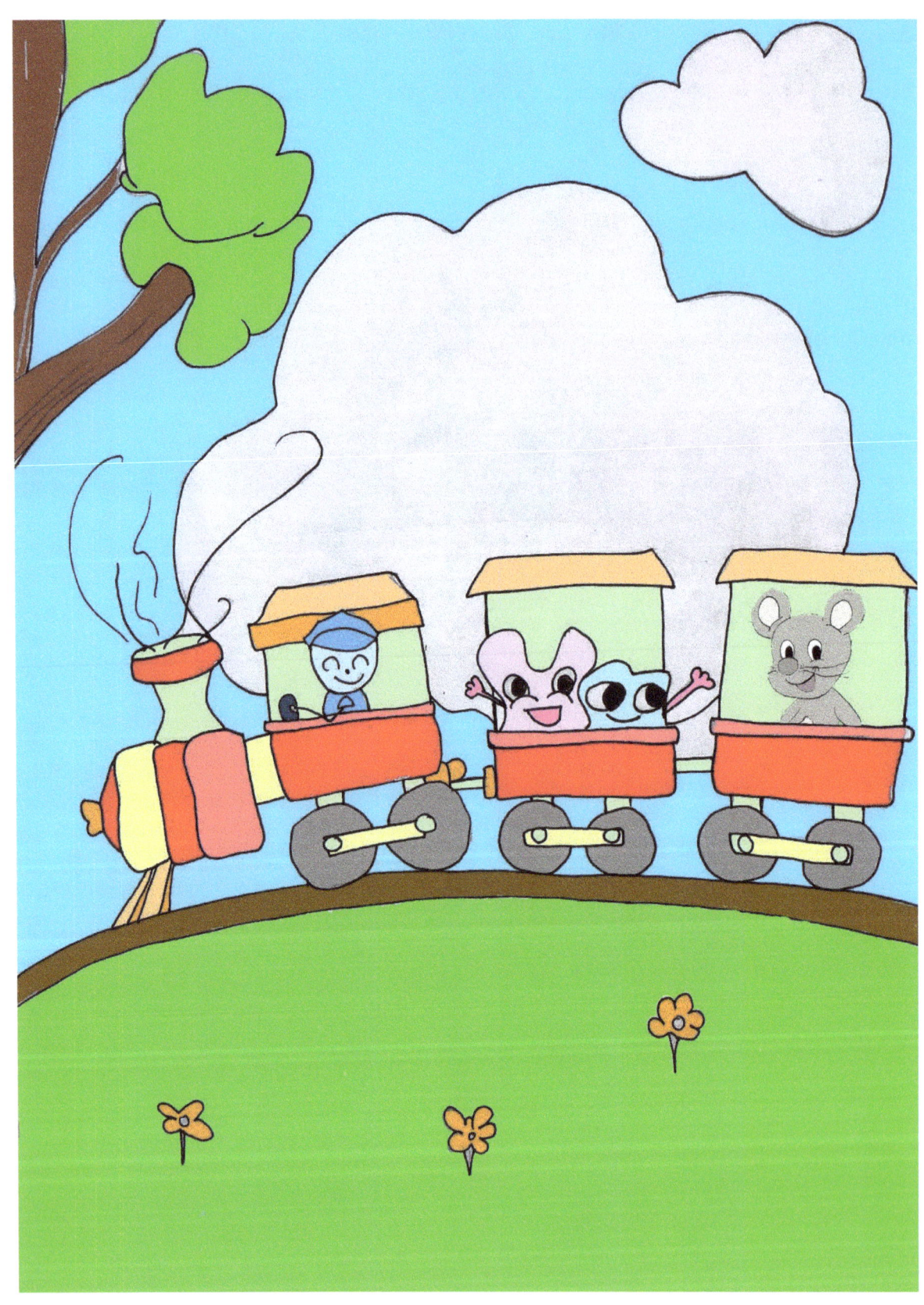

Little Mr Mouse, Bob and Sam jumped onto the train. The four of them then headed over to Big Town. By this time, it was the afternoon, and everyone were waiting. The train with its chimney smoke set about making loads of different wonderful shapes.

Town Land enjoyed them selfies ever so much and the day was a great success.

Home Cooking

Concrete Cooker was at home in Big Town cooking for his best chum Friendly Fork. Everything was going along smoothly. Until Concrete Cooker broke down.

"What do we do now?" Friendly wondered.

"I'll have to go around to Mini's house to get help."

Concrete Cooker then set out to Mini Microwave Man's house, "Mini can you help me, I was cooking for Friendly and I broke down?"

"No problem. Can my friends join us?"

"Of course."

PTO

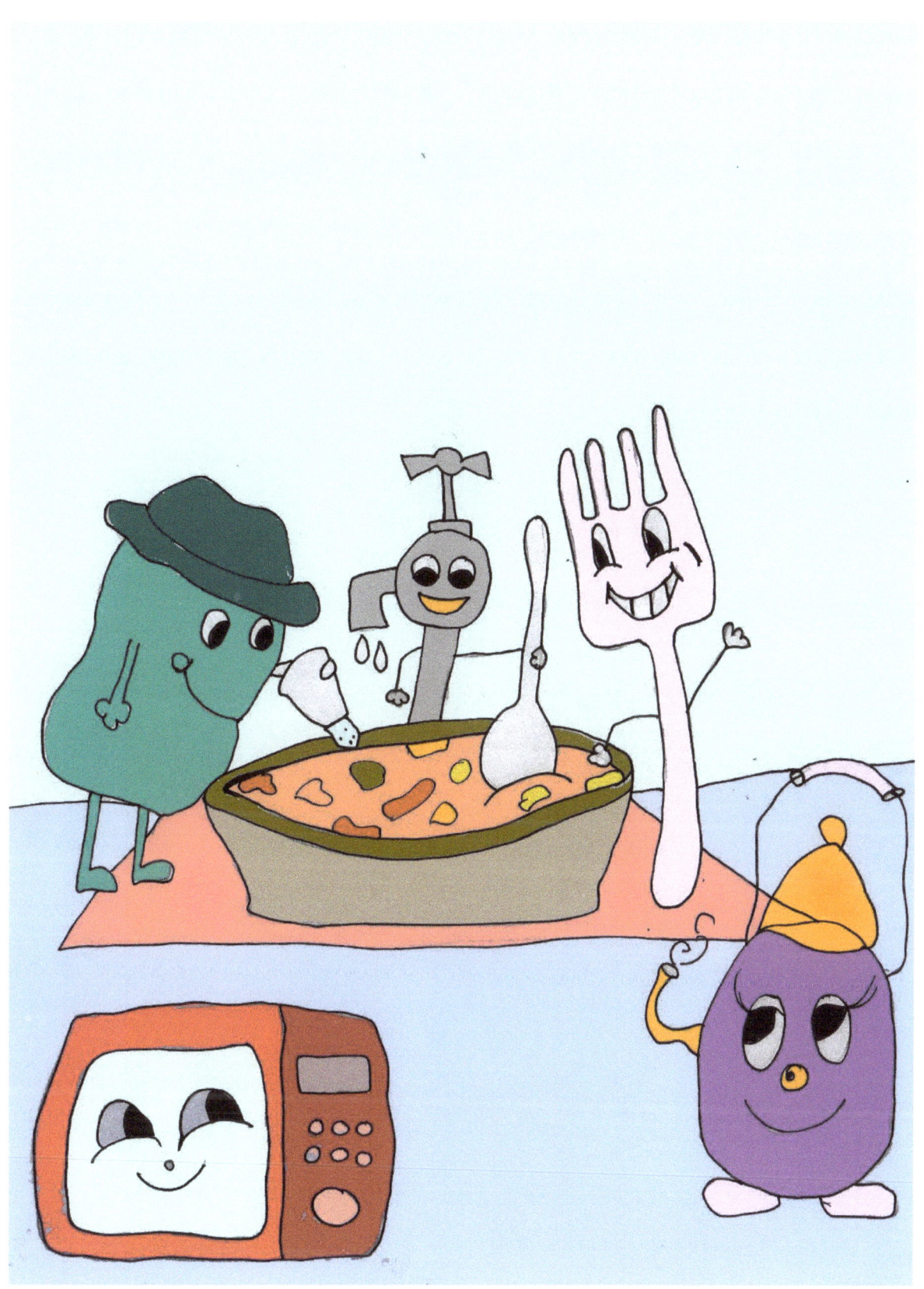

Concrete Cooker, Mini Microwave Man, Terry Tap, Paper Towel Man and Kylie the Kettle Lady set off back to where, Friendly Fork was waiting. Then when they all arrived Mini cooked the food that Cooker could not cook.

After dinner Paper Towel Man wiped his friend's mouths. Terry Tap helped wash up. Friendly Fork helped everyone eat. Kylie the Kettle Lady also helped make coffee before it was too late to go to bed.

Who is this?

It was a lovely day in Big Town. Bibby as usual was skimming stones at the Big Pond. Soon though, after a day of skimming, he was just about to get the surprise of his life. The sun was beginning to go down and Bibby was starting to get tired.

Bibby skimmed what he thought was his last stone of the night. As he did so he could see someone or something walking towards the Pond from the other side. He stood up. Scared he tried to work out who or what was heading towards him. He shouted, "Who's that?" A voice from the other side of the Pond shouted back.

"Who's that?" Bibby noticed straight away that it was a voice he had not heard before.

Bibby stood watching. Hoping that whoever it was would come into sight because it was so dark. "What's your name?" Bibby said. "My name is Bibby Girl." The voice replied.

"Are you lost?" Bibby said as he began to walk round to where the voice was coming from. Bibby Girl did not answer. As Bibby got to the other side slowly Bibby Girl started to come into view.

PTO

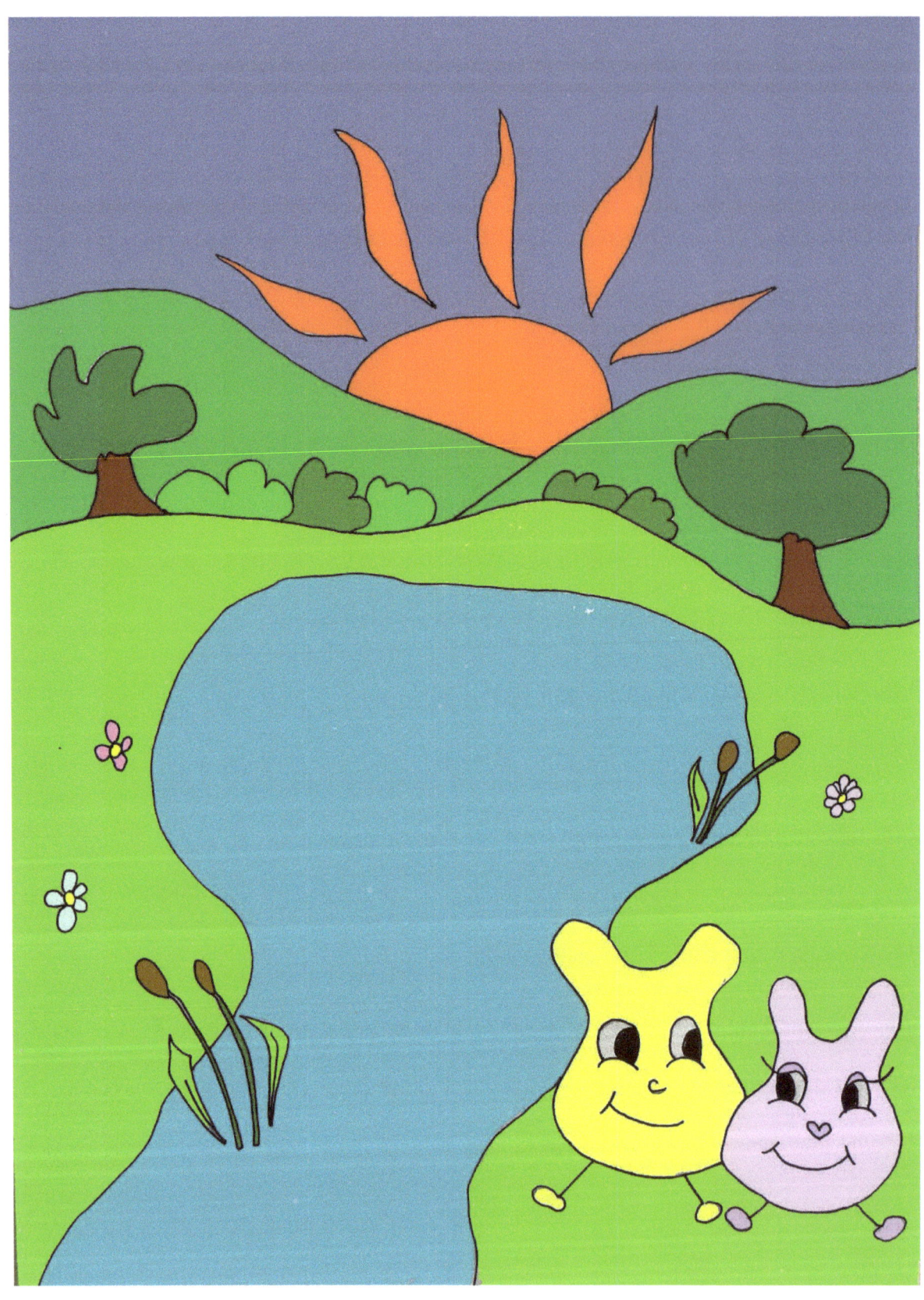

By the time Bibby could see Bibby Girl the sun had almost gone down. They started to talk as the sun disappeared, sitting down next to each other they began to skim stones. The two then talked and talked all night long until morning came the next day.

The End